Life and Death in the North Woods

The Story of the Maine Game Warden Service

ERIC WIGHT

Down East Books

CAMDEN, MAINE

Published by Down East Books

A wholly owned subsidiary of the Rowman and Littlefield Publishing Group, Inc.

4501 Forbes Boulevard, Suite 200, Lanham, Maryland 20706

www.rowman.com

16 Carlisle Street, London W1D 3BT, United Kingdom

Distributed by National Book Network

Originally published in 1985 by the DeLorme Publishing Company

First Down East Books edition 2014

British Library Cataloguing in Publication Information Available

Library of Congress Cataloging-in-Publication Data Available

ISBN 978-1-60893-331-0 (pbk. : alk. paper)

ISBN 978-1-60893-332-7 (electronic)

♾™ The paper used in this publication meets the minimum requirements of American National Standard for Information Sciences Permanence of Paper for Printed Library Materials, ANSI/NISO Z39.48-1992.

Printed in the United States of America

Dedicated to the memory of my younger brother Kevin, with whom I hiked many a mountain trail and snow-mobiled many a mile.

ACKNOWLEDGMENTS

I would like to express my heartfelt thanks to my wife Karen, who spent many hours at a typewriter converting my scribblings into legible form, and to my son Nathan, who created the illustration for the first page of this book. I would also like to thank my fellow wardens, both active and retired, who contributed their time, materials, and thoughts for this book. And a special thank-you to the Department of Inland Fisheries and Wildlife, which furnished so many photographs.

CONTENTS

INTRODUCTION

By Rob Sneddon

Questions. Always with the questions.

"If I stop for any reason," says Maine Game Warden Neal Wykes of Naples, "someone will come up and ask me something within five minutes."

It goes with the territory—which is considerable. Wykes's beat, Wildlife Management District 15, stretches roughly from the White Mountain National Forest to Auburn, then southwest through Limington and Limerick to Newfield.

As Wykes arrives at Sebago Lake to begin a routine patrol, he notes that "there's no [other game warden] between here and New Hampshire except for me. And there's a lot of water. My district covers the northern end of Sebago Lake all the way up through the Songo River into Long Lake. And on top of that, I've got another fifteen bodies of water. I might not even get to every body of water over a summer."

Wykes also has to cover a lot of ground, too, when it comes to his responsibilities. In addition to its never-ending pursuit of poachers the Warden Service also handles everything from catch-and-release of nuisance animals to checking boats for compliance with Maine's strict invasive-milfoil statutes, to search-and-rescue for missing children.

Suffice it to say that the Warden Service's numbers are insufficient for such a sprawling mission (just ninety-five full-time game wardens). "It's getting to the point where we're so overwhelmed with everything else that we just have to squeeze [hunting and fishing enforcement] in whenever we can," Wykes says.

Now factor in the average citizen's sketchy understanding of the laws of nature, both literal and figurative, and the Warden Service's ambiguous place in the enforcement hierarchy, and the public's curiosity makes perfect sense. "People have questions that they've wondered about for a while but they never knew who to ask," Wykes says. "Or they didn't know how to get a hold of a game warden. A lot of people just don't know where to find us."

It's not that the Maine Warden Service operates in secrecy. Or at least that wasn't the intent. It's just that the service has continually evolved since it was conceived as a sort of "green police" 130 years ago. The market for wild fish and game was much greater then than it is now, and many out-of-state visitors plundered Maine's woods and waters for profit. Mainers responded with some of the country's earliest conservation laws. Wrote a *New York Times* angling columnist in 1876: "Your correspondent has been greatly surprised at the superior intelligence with which the Maine people are caring for their sporting-ground," adding with obvious envy that Maine had already taken steps to "prevent the causeless destruction which goes on in our New York lakes and woods."

Enforcing Maine's conservation laws was a big job then, and it has only grown bigger with time. "From the beginning, when we just dealt with moose and deer [poachers], our mission has grown just because of the recreational opportunities that Maine offers off-road," says John MacDonald, a Warden Service corporal.

"Any hunting or fishing opportunities, any motorized [off-road] vehicles, all of that falls under our jurisdiction for safety and enforcement. And hiking has become so popular with the Appalachian Trail. People can get lost. It's our responsibility to manage those searches, at least when they get large.

"We've really developed a niche in search-and-rescue. It's not just hikers and hunters and people who fish, it's Alzheimer's patients who may have wandered from nursing homes—even missing persons and fugitives."

But by far the biggest change in the Warden Service since it formally began on March 9, 1880, involves oversight of recreational vehicles. In 2008, the Warden Service issued more summonses for snowmobile violations than for anything else: 847. For context, the service issued just twenty-nine summonses for trapping violations.

The disproportionate number of snowmobile citations is due in part to an increase in wintertime patrols along the border with Canada since the Department of Homeland Security was formed. But it's also a function of simple mathematics. Maine has an estimated 13,000 miles of snow trails, which attract upward of 100,000 snow machines each winter. Says MacDonald, "Really, we could focus all of our time on snowmobiles."

Or ATVs. Or boats. A paradox applies to recreational vehicles. In many ways, they're more dangerous than automobiles—and yet the laws that govern them are more lax. For whatever reason, people think that there should be fewer rules of the road when there is no road. That makes safety enforcement a challenge. A sixth-grade girl could pilot a beefy bass boat across Sebago Lake at full throttle while her parents sip cocktails in the stern, and that family would be breaking no laws. There's no open-container law for watercraft, no open-water speed limit, and kids as young as twelve are allowed to operate motorboats without restriction. Ten-year-olds can legally operate snowmobiles and ATVs, and while children between ten and sixteen are supposed to complete an ATV safety training course and ride only when accompanied by an adult, that doesn't always happen.

So it's no surprise that accidents often do happen. And when they do, preserving and reconstructing the scene can be difficult. "A lot of times with recreational vehicle [accidents] it's hard to determine speeds because they don't take place on roads, where you'd have clearly defined skidmarks," says MacDonald, a member of the Warden Service's forensic mapping team. "With a snowmobile, it could be snowing [and the scene gets covered] or it could be warm and the scene melts. And if it's a boat crash, everything floats away or sinks. So [forensic mapping] actually helps us record boat accidents a lot better. If we find debris on the bottom we'll set up something on the surface directly above it so we can map [the accident scene] just like we would on land."

The Warden Service has evolved with the times in its investigation of conventional poaching cases, too. DNA testing has become routine. "I had a case five or six years ago where a guy killed six deer and didn't register any of them," MacDonald says. "Without that technology I really wouldn't have been able to prove that he had six different deer. He could have told me it was just one deer—just a lot of it. But [DNA testing] can distinguish one deer from the next."

Back at Sebago Lake, Neal Wykes still hasn't made it from his state-issued Ford F-250 Super Duty to his boat to begin his patrol. Yet another person has approached him with yet another question. A man with a cartoonishly thick New York accent is taking his nine-year-old son fishing. Maine residents under sixteen and non-residents under twelve may fish without a license, but the father wants to know if he needs a license just to accompany his son.

The short answer is no. But after nearly thirty years as a warden, Wykes knows that short answers are often inadequate. So, displaying the deftness that helped make him the 2006 Maine Warden of the Year, Wykes probes for a little more information. His tone is calm, conversational. How many rods will they be using? Just one. Will the boy actually be doing everything himself? Yes, the man says. Then he dangles a qualifier. "But you know how nine-year-olds are. Sometimes they get bored and wander off."

"Well," Wykes says after a pause, "if your son's not with you and you're standing there with a line in the water—you're fishing."

He doesn't tell the man that he needs a license. He just helps the man make an informed decision.

A moment later Wykes gets a call on his state-issued cell phone. He grabs a yellow pad and a Bic pen, the lowest-tech pieces of equipment in his truck, which is outfitted with a laptop computer and a GPS, along with a conventional police radio, emergency lights, and siren. There's also plenty of stuff specific to the Warden Service's mission, such as a decibel meter to help enforce the noise limit for powerboats.

And, like every full-time member of the Maine Warden Service, Wykes is armed. He carries a shotgun in the back of the truck and a SIG Sauer P226 .357-caliber semi-automatic handgun at his side.

Maine's first game wardens had to supply their own guns. They received no training, no special equipment—not even a salary. Wardens, an 1881 report from Maine's Commissioners of Fisheries and Game noted, "are expected to be sustained by enthusiasm alone in game protection, to abandon home and the occupations that give bread to their families, and go forth to the forest for one half the penalties they may obtain from captured and convicted law breakers, and the soul stirring privilege of shooting at sight any dog they may discover chasing deer."

That high-horse directive invited confrontation. And backwoods Maine in the nineteenth century teemed with tough customers willing to accept the invitation. If contemporaneous accounts are to be believed, parts of the state were a sort of Down East Wild West—the town of Wesley in particular. An 1886 *Boston Globe* article described Wesley as having "a turbulent spirit," and asserted that the town "had retained, amid many good citizens, some of the lawless sort." Those lawless sorts had recently proposed that the town vote to nullify state game laws. The motion passed.

The *Globe* article, citing the Lewiston Journal as its source, included a harrowing account of a Maine game warden's attempt to exercise the "soul-stirring privilege" of shooting a poacher's dogs. "If [the warden] can't draw the dogs away from the owners so as to poison them," the Journal noted, "he waits until night when the men and the dogs have gone into camp. Stealing up softly, he flashes his dark lantern on the sleeper, and shoots down the dogs. He cannot arrest the poachers in the middle of the wilderness and drag them out single-handed, but he takes their names and arrests them when he gets a good chance.

"Everybody can see the danger in this business. The men, sleeping there with those dogs, have no fine moral scruples and would not feel very bad if a bullet from one of their guns should bore a hole in a game warden."

In November 1886 the inevitable happened. Wardens Lyman O. Hill, of Machias, and Charles W. Niles, of Wesley, were gunned down at Fletcher Brook while trying to seize a suspected poacher's dog.

Hill and Niles were the first two of fourteen members of the Maine Warden Service killed in the line of duty—the most of any branch of Maine law enforcement.

Both society and the Warden Service have come a long way since the 1880s. Nevertheless, says Corporal MacDonald, "We still have a handful of [violent encounters] each year. A lot of times the [suspect] is a convicted felon or they're on probation, or maybe they're growing marijuana and we get in the middle of that.

"But I think most people have a pretty high respect for game wardens. Most [poachers], when they've been caught, they just give it up. But then again, most of the people we encounter are sportsmen and -women, and most carry weapons of some type. And [given] the remoteness of where we check them, it probably runs through [a criminal's] mind that they could get away with trying to escape, more than they might on a highway [stop]."

Today, all wardens must complete Basic Law Enforcement Training Program at the Maine Criminal Justice Academy in Vassalboro. Wardens then receive an additional fourteen weeks of intensive training in techniques specific to the Warden Service, including a full week on search-and-rescue.

Improved safety has come in a slow, steady succession of steps, many of which seem obvious in hindsight. For one, wardens are no longer encouraged to shoot dogs.

For another, all wardens must know how to swim. That's

been a requirement only since 1972. That September, Warden Richard Varney died when his helicopter crashed in Maranacook Lake. Varney, who didn't know how to swim, survived the crash but drowned in eight feet of water.

The Warden Service has benefited from exponential advances in equipment, too. Last February, Warden Gary Allen survived a plunge through the ice at Sebago Lake on an ATV. He was wearing a "float coat," a Mustang survival snowmobile jacket filled with flotation material. "He said there was no question in his mind that the coat saved his life," Neal Wykes says. "He went completely under—even his snowmobile helmet filled with water. Next thing he knew, he popped right back up on the surface."

Wykes relates this story just before he boards his patrol boat, which is kept at a slip at the Point Sebago Resort. The boat, built by SAFE Boats International of Port Orchard, Washington, is an unnamed Coast Guard-style "T-Type" twenty-five-footer outfitted with twin Mercury 250-horsepower motors. Top of the line, in other words.

First impression of a routine Warden Service patrol of Sebago Lake: It's fun. And Wykes confirms that it can be. But, he adds, "It's not so fun being out here in the middle of a raging thunderstorm, looking for someone who didn't know enough to come in."

To look at Sebago Lake through Wykes' eyes is to feel an almost paralyzing sense of responsibility. Danger lurks everywhere. And its prospective victims are often oblivious. Clueless Jet-Skiers who stare dumbly in response to the words "headway speed." Kayakers who rationalize their potentially lethal negligence with a non sequitur: I don't need a life jacket because I don't have a motor. Or, as Wykes puts it, "The people most likely not to have life jackets are the people in boats that are most likely to tip over." And on and on.

And that's one lake on a quiet morning. Consider all the other lakes and ponds and rivers and streams, to say nothing of the hills and valleys and meadows and woods, stretched from here to New Hampshire, harboring creatures as small as black flies and as big as black bears. Now imagine that it's up to you, and you alone, to not only protect all that from desecration, but also to keep people safe as they blunder through it, many with an ignorance that borders on the criminal.

You can only imagine how stressful that must be. And you can only imagine how many people can thank the Maine Warden Service for their lives. And yet a segment of the public still perceives game wardens as overofficious Barney Fifes intent on ruining people's fun.

Even those who try to be respectful often do so in a backhanded way. After Wykes finishes his patrol, he's walking back to his truck when he gets another one of those questions. A young man is considering a career in law enforcement. He wants to know how to get started. And this is how he broaches the subject with Neal Wykes, an armed, uniformed, and expertly trained graduate of the Maine Criminal Justice Academy who has placed himself in significant danger time and again in his three decades of public service: "I know you're not really a cop, but . . . ."

In almost thirty years as a Maine Game Warden, Neal Wykes has had hundreds of encounters with nuisance animals—including some toothy visitors.

Maine Game Warden Neal Wykes devotes a significant portion of his time to nuisance-animal calls. In many cases the callers are a greater nuisance than the animals. "You can never really trust what you get for a call," Wykes says. "A lot of people are just very uneducated about wildlife."

For instance, there was the time Wykes received a call about an injured eagle—a high priority, given the eagle's threatened status. "I get there," Wykes says, "and it's a partridge. You wonder: How did this turn into an eagle? You know those [callers] aren't from Maine."

Wykes says people from away account for many such wild goose—or partridge—chases. "They move up here from Connecticut or New York—from an area that I'd be scared to death to live in," Wykes says. "And they're scared to death because there's a porcupine walking through their backyard. So they call us."

Wykes laughs. "It's entertaining. At times."

The strangest visitor that Wykes ever encountered came from much farther away than New Hampshire.

"I got a call that there was an alligator in the farm pond at the Maine Audubon Society in Yarmouth," Wykes says. "I said, 'Yeah, right.' But it was very much real."

Wykes guesses that the alligator, which was about three feet long, was a pet that had simply grown too big to handle safely. Earlier this year, the Warden Service fielded a similar call about a Gaboon viper behind the Cinemagic theater in Saco.

The snake died. The alligator was more fortunate. "I think [the owner] purposely put it in the Audubon pond knowing that it would be properly taken care of," says Wykes, who helped recover the alligator.

It was early spring, which made the gator rescue easier. "A guy with a wet suit just picked it up and brought it out because the cold had rendered it essentially motionless," Wykes says.

Before being transported to Wild Animal Kingdom in York, the gator spent the night in a pet carrier—indoors. "That was a whole different alligator in the morning," Wykes says. "He'd warned up, and he was sommme nasty. There was no holding onto him at that point."

The air temperature was still cool enough that the alligator had mellowed again by the time it had completed the trip to York in the bed of Wykes' truck.

While Wykes has relocated many a bear and even an alligator without incident, he's been less fortunate with skunks. Typically, trouble starts when Wykes tries to live-trap a nuisance raccoon. "Skunks always seem to beat the 'coon to the feed," he says. "And you find out just how far their spray can actually reach. It's twenty to twenty-five feet, and highly accurate."

Adds Wykes, "I've been full-blown sprayed about three times. And it only takes once to gain a lot of respect for a skunk."

1 — WHO ARE THOSE GUYS?

The only thing I can think of that beats living in the State of Maine has to be—living in the State of Maine as a game warden. I am sure that a lot of people must agree with the first part of that statement; as for the second part, well, that may take a little convincing, or at least some sort of explanation, which is what this book will attempt to do. Remember an oft-repeated line from the motion picture *Butch Cassidy and the Sundance Kid,* as each time the title characters looked back, dismayed at their failure to elude their pursuers, and said, "Who are those guys, anyway?" In this story, "those guys" are the game wardens.

Our story is about how and why we came to be, and how we have progressed since those early days. Some of these tales are funny and others not so funny, but all of them are true. They describe how we game wardens live—and in some cases, have died—in the line of duty for a cause that we believe in very deeply.

At the writing of this book, I have been a game warden for exactly half my life—twenty-one and a half years. Now, granted, that longevity does not rank me with the pyramids, but it has put me in contact with almost every type of situation a game warden can experience, I guess, either directly or through hearsay.

Apparently, many folks think a game warden has some mysterious power to appear or disappear at will. I certainly would not want to dispel that notion, but perhaps an explanation would help.

Someone in wildlife circles was quoted as saying that the coyote is the least-understood animal in Maine. Now, if a sociologist were to make this same statement in regard to people, he would probably be talking about game wardens.

It's really not all that mysterious. First of all, a game warden is deeply committed to his job—all aspects of it. Then, because he spends much of his time in the woods, he becomes very much at home in that atmosphere. He studies people's habits, knows where certain types of people are apt to be and what they will be doing. He has a deeper understanding of nature than most, because he deals with it in all its phases—good and bad, season to season—year in, year out. He knows where different animals live and where they are most apt to be at certain times. And so, considering his acquired "woods sense" and tracking skills, you really shouldn't be too bowled over when he suddenly steps out in front of you when you thought no one was around. A good game warden is no more mysterious than a good carpenter who uses shortcuts to make his job easier. But people, when checked by a warden, will wonder, "How the hell did he know I was here?," or, "Where did he come from, anyway?"

As for the world's first warden—where did *he* come from? His evolution, I suspect, was like this: First came the first game law, second came the first poacher, then came the warden.

It is known that in ancient Greece, deer poachers suffered capital punishment. Later, in England, King Henry VIII was quite the sport, and he reportedly revamped the existing game laws of England. Falconry was his sport, and so he made the possession of one hawk egg punishable by death. (I would not say he was all that good a sport!) At any rate, someone in history must have enforced these laws to some extent and made an attempt to curtail or apprehend violators, and it is from these roots that today's game wardens have come. From the English gamekeepers who looked after the King's deer in Sherwood Forest, to Maine's game wardens, to African game protectors trying to stop the extermination of the rhinoceros, their job is basically the same all over the world.

A game warden's job is frequently referred to as *not a job, but a way of life.* There is no question that this is true. Wardens everywhere share this enthusiasm and dedication toward their job. Most other jobs are fairly routine in that the hours are set; you know when you will be at home or at work, and can make personal plans accordingly. By contrast, much of a warden's work is surveillance. He sits and watches, and waits for something to happen. It may not happen today or tonight, but he'll be back again tomorrow night, just hoping to apprehend someone killing a deer, dipping smelts in a closed brook, shooting alligators in closed season, butchering a rhino for his horn. He feels good, having helped save an animal or having apprehended someone trying to steal something from everyone—including himself. He is run by self-generating dedication and enthusiasm—not by clocks that dictate when to go to work, get up, go home, eat lunch. A warden's career might be described as a continuous game of wits with other people—not unlike a chess game, with the ultimate objective being conservation of fish and game that belong to everyone. It is a game of inches and seconds. Sometimes he wins, sometimes he loses, but the warden keeps going back to try again.

As we look at how Maine Warden Service evolved, I think it helps to take a look at the state itself. The first thing you'll notice is its immenseness. When the boundaries were finally established, we had a piece of real estate 310 miles long and 210 miles wide. This makes Maine's area 33,040 square miles, only 215 square miles less in area than the other five New England states combined. This territory includes 2,465 lakes, with a combined area of approximately 3,200 square miles of water surface, and four long navigable rivers, plus 5,147 streams and small rivers. When Maine is broken down into terrain types, we find approximately 15,000,000 acres of forest and 4,000,000 acres of farmland. You can now begin to comprehend the size of the army it would take to enforce, to any extent, regulations dealing with fish and game.

Early on in Maine's history, there was not any attempt at this sort of thing. Much of the state was still uninhabited. For the most part, the population dwelt along the rivers upstream from the ocean, as well as along the coast itself. Following Maine's admittance to the Union in 1820, a few laws were passed dealing primarily with the method of taking a fish along the tidal river mouths and bays.

As the state's population grew, these laws involving fish were expanded to include freshwater species also, and, along with some unpaid men called fish wardens, were Maine's first attempt at conservation. Fish were still abundant everywhere, and most people saw no cause for alarm; therefore, compliance was very limited. The Department of Inland Fisheries was established in 1850. As for hunting, there had been game laws regulating the seasons since 1830, but since there was no bag limit, no enforcement was attempted. The first attempt at enforcing any game laws came (as near as I can tell) in the mid-1860s, when the legislature authorized seven counties to appoint moose wardens. These men, I am afraid, met with very limited success, and received anywhere from $25 to $85 per year, depending on the apprehensions they made.

Following the Civil War and into the 1870s, things noticeably began to change. Game was abundant in most of the state, and some individuals began to capitalize to a great extent on this fact. Moose, caribou, and deer were being market-hunted and shipped by the hundreds by rail to points south. This was viewed by many as wrong, but nothing could be done. The sixty wardens who were employed to enforce the fishery laws were not empowered to protect game. Worse, there were not really many laws to enforce regarding game. In many cases, these animals—especially deer—were killed by men with packs of dogs. This is a very effective method of hunting deer, especially when a water barrier is present. Men stationed along the shore or in boats killed everything that the dogs drove to water. Although a law was passed in 1873 which reduced the bag limit to three deer per year and the season had undergone several alterations, there still was no enforcement. The only way to prosecute an individual was if a concerned citizen was willing to come forth. He could, on presentation of a sworn affidavit, have a person brought before the court. Most citizens were reluctant, for good reason: During this time, several fish wardens had been attacked, beaten, and, in one case, left unconscious by gangs of salmon poachers. Understandably, very few private individuals were concerned enough to take the risk.

For several years during this period, the various commissioners in the Department of Inland Fisheries had pleaded with Legislature to extend the powers of fish wardens to include enforcement of game laws as well. The reason for their refusal is age-old: There simply was no money. Finally, in 1880, after several years of work, the following bill was introduced. When it passed, the Maine Warden Service was born.

Chapter 208

An act to enlarge the powers and duties of the Commissioners of Fisheries, and Wardens.

Be it enacted by the Senate and House Representatives in Legislature assembled, as follows:

SECT. I. The powers and duties of the commissioners of fisheries, and wardens, shall extend to all matters pertaining to game, and they shall have the same powers to enforce all laws pertaining to game as they now have in enforcing the laws relating to the fisheries.

SECT. 2. The governor is hereby authorized, with the advice and consent of the council, to appoint wardens, whose duty it shall be to enforce the provisions of all laws relating to game and the fisheries, arrest any person violating such laws, and prosecute for all offenses against the same that may come to their knowledge; and shall have the same power as sheriffs and deputy sheriffs, to serve all criminal processes for violations of the provisions of any law pertaining to game and the fisheries, and shall be allowed for said services the same fees as are prescribed by law for sheriffs and their deputies for like services; and in the execution of their duties they shall have the same right to require aid that sheriffs and their deputies have in executing the duties of their office; and any person refusing or neglecting to render such aid when required, shall forfeit ten dollars, to be recovered upon complaint before any trial justice or municipal court.

SECT. 3. This act shall take effect when approved.

Approved March 9, 1880.

The first action resulted three days following the approval of the law, on March 12, 1880, when two men were apprehended killing a doe deer in closed season. Upon conviction, they paid fines total-ing $71. The die was cast.

Our first years as an organization were like the infancy of most anything else: We stumbled around for several years with no real sense of direction. The problems were many and varied. The most distressing aspect of it all was that there was no money to pay war-dens. These sixty fish wardens who now had taken on game laws as well still had only the annual $1,500 that originally had been appropriated for their pay. Another problem was that these men still lived nearer the coast and could not effectively enforce laws inland without leaving home, sometimes for lengthy spells.

A good friend to the Warden Service was Commissioner Henry Stanley from Dixfield. Stanley served as a commissioner for thirty-four years, and continuously tried to improve the Warden Service with appeals for more money. An example of his efforts in our behalf appeared in his annual report to the governor in 1881. He stated the following: "Game wardens receive no regular salary at all. They are expected to be sustained by enthusiasm alone in game protection; to abandon home and the occupations that give bread to their families, and go forth to the forest for the reward of one-half of the penalties that they may obtain from captured and convicted law-breakers and the soul-stirring privilege of shooting on sight any dog which they may observe chasing deer." I suppose the governor got a chuckle or two from that—I certainly did—but many a truth is spoken in jest. Men were understandably reluctant to make sacrifices for such meager reimbursement. You must also remember that these first wardens were, first of all, private citizens with jobs or farms who only did warden work on occasions when time allowed. They received half of the fine upon the conviction, the other half going to the overseer of the poor in the town where the prosecutor lived.

Improvements were very slow in coming, but eventually things began to tighten up. People engaged in illegal activities began to realize that now they could be caught. One of the first examples was the problem regarding the wholesale slaughter of Maine moose along the Québec boundary. This had gone on for years, with no attempt made to stop it. In 1883, a law prohibiting the exportation of game from Maine was passed. This law put an end to the railcars of deer and caribou being shipped from Maine each year. It also had a tremendous effect on the number of illegally taken Maine moose, the hides of which had found their way to the Toronto market each year. The Canadians who made forays into Maine each spring to hunt moose had been given the name "crusters," the reason being that they came when the snow had formed a crust, and getting around was best for them and worse for the moose. During the twenty years following our formation, the groundwork was being laid for future game wardens. Laws were now being passed every year dealing with fish and game in an effort to conserve. The department was well into the management aspect of fish and game by virtue of an 1882 law.

Still, there were not enough wardens to act as a really effective deterrent. There were hundreds of lumber camps around the state, with thousands of men to be fed daily during the winter. The law did not prohibit the serving of deer meat in these camps, but it must have been stretched somewhat in regards to the three-per-year bag limit per person. Most camps had one full-time hunter, and some larger ones had two or three. Wardens spent a good deal of their time, in winter, in and around these camps, checking on this type of activity. Understandably, they were not always welcome, and it often meant sleeping outside or in some primitive trapper's shack to make sure their presence was undetected.

Being a warden was by no means a popular job in those days. Many wardens received threats of bodily harm, and some received worse treatment. Places in the woods where wardens sometimes stayed were known to catch fire from time to time.

It was during this same period that Maine began to be recognized by others as having the most rigid and best-enforced fish and game regulations anywhere.

As we look at the development of the Maine Warden Service, certain events seem to have played important roles. Until the 1900s, the department and its wardens were not widely known. At this point in the story, licenses were not required for fishing or hunting, so no money was coming to the department from that angle. Lack of funds was still the obstacle to hiring good, reliable men as wardens. Besides, other types of outdoor employment were available to these same men, with rewards that were far better in monetary terms.

Maine had blossomed into the fish-and-game capital of the East, and by 1900, recreational sporting was in full swing. Sportsmen from everywhere, mostly out of state, flocked to the hundreds of sporting camps, but they contributed nothing to state coffers. Guides were in great demand then, and the pay was substantially better than that of a game warden. A guide was earning $3 per day then, and a game warden, $2 per day. Many wardens went into guiding; at one point, there were only forty-eight wardens statewide. Then came the first real step. (Well, it was actually a half-step and a trip, but at least it was a forward motion.)

In 1899, a law called "The September Law" was passed—an

extremely controversial law, but the first attempt for a license program. It provided that upon payment of $4 by a resident, and $6 by a nonresident, a deer could be taken in September. The money was wonderful, but the problems created were not, such as a rather large rift that appeared between residents and nonresidents: Many residents felt the nonresidents were not charged enough. (This all has a familiar ring to it, somehow.) Also, as was discovered the hard way, a trophy hunter would sometimes kill a buck and hide the carcass. Later, when he got a bigger deer, he would burn the first one in a brush pile to destroy the evidence, and on several such occasions, a forest fire was started as a result. At any rate, the September Law did not have the desired effect—that being, to raise money for the department—and the law, due to its extreme unpopularity, was abolished fairly quickly.

The first significant move in regard to improving the Warden Service came in 1904. It was then that nonresidents were required to purchase a hunting license for $15. Other licenses were to follow, but this first one helped the Warden Service expand to provide better coverage and better pay. One of the first tasks accomplished with the money was the building of six new warden camps along the Québec boundary, and wardens were stationed there, two to a camp (for safety reasons). From then on, our service began to grow—but a very slow growth it was. It was still difficult to keep a good man in a remote area, simply because of the low pay and hardships involved. It was not something a family man could usually endure. The equipment provided was minimal; if you were lucky, you might have a canoe.

Nevertheless, from time to time, as money would allow, more wardens were hired. A major setback came with World War I.

Many wardens left for active duty, and although some reentered the Warden Service upon return, many did not. Then, in 1922, due to lack of funds, half the wardens were laid off. (That, too, has somewhat of a familiar ring. In more recent years, because of a similar problem, wardens were once asked to work for half-pay for several months.) As a group, our mettle has been severely tested several times, and I suspect that we who have come later have benefited from the perseverance and dedication of those who held up under those dark days years ago.

The Maine Warden Service was on its feet by around 1930. By then, things had fallen into place somewhat, and a soundly structured organization had evolved.

It is definitely not a coincidence that this stability arrived while a man named George Stobie served as commissioner. Among the older warden retirees are several who can remember the man well, and they are quick to point out that it was he who got us headed in the right direction. George Stobie served as commissioner of Inland Fish and Game from 1928 to 1950. His insight, as well as his generosity, came into play many times during his tenure.

Apparently, he had deep feelings about what the Warden Service should be, and on many occasions was not bashful about spending his own money to acquire a much-needed piece of equipment for the men in the field. Retired supervisor Arthur Rogers recalls that when his father passed away, Mr. Stobie called him in and took money from his own pocket so that Arthur might buy train fare to attend his dad's funeral. Stobie was as practical as he was generous. Retired warden Leon Wilson, who went to work at Nine Mile District on the St. John River in 1932, told me that when he went to work, Mr. Stobie gave him his only instructions.

He handed Leon a law book and said, "Leon, half of your job lies between the pages of this book. The other half lies from your ears up."

It was George Stobie who got aircraft involved in the Warden Service, made sure they became a fixture, and that the program expanded. (I will include more on him and airplanes later on.)

From an organizational standpoint, we began to really shape up under Stobie's tutelage. The Maine Warden Service was divided into four zones at this time, with one so-called "Chief Warden" in the North Zone and one in the South Zone. These two men were just what Stobie wanted.

W. B. Small, the northern chief from Farmington, had been a sheriff for quite some time prior to joining the Warden Service. His southern counterpart was Joseph Stickney from Saco, who also had a law enforcement background. George Stobie felt that these two men had the capability to bond the Warden Service together in a common cause if a stronger emphasis were placed on law enforcement and training, and he was right. The first warden schools they set up were successful, and continue to this day.

I would like to make further note in regard to Joe Stickney. Joe was a very well-known fly fisherman in his day. He is credited with several flies, among them the "Supervisor" and the "Lady Doctor," named for his wife, Dr. Laura Black Stickney.

W. B. (Bert) Small apparently was no slouch, either. Helon Taylor recalls that Small had a bullet scar on his cheek received on a domestic call as sheriff. Helon also told me about the time Small snowshoed all the way to the headwaters of Kibby Stream to arrest a man for murder. The man, when arrested, refused to walk out, and insisted on having a horse and sleigh come to carry him out. Small handcuffed him to a tree and said, "Fine, I'll be back in two days with the sleigh." "Never mind, I'll walk," said the man.

I hope I have conveyed just how influential George Stobie was in our development. He was a great, tall man, admired by employees as well as the sporting public for his efforts in fish and game matters. His regard for wardens is best illustrated, I think, in the following comment that he included in his annual report to the governor in 1932: "Every warden is provided with fish and game laws, and, of course, is expected to familiarize himself with them. These laws reflect the policy of the State, but the warden should look beyond the letter of the law and catch the vision of their spirit. Wardens are not just fish and game protectors. They are much more than that. They are the State personified."

We certainly take our hats off to that man.

It would appear that the Maine Warden Service reached full stride in the late 1950s. And, along with the strengthening of our organization and its effectiveness, we now had a snappy uniform that had undergone several changes.

Uniforms help inspire respect, I suppose, but they often are not completely desirable from a working point of view; besides, mud and burrs do not enhance the looks of anything, as a rule. Our original uniform, issued in 1934, was—to my way of thinking—very sharp-looking. It consisted of a hat and jacket, along with shirt and tie, and trousers that were riding-breeches style, worn with high leather boots. Actually, wardens had a choice of wearing the high boots, or shoes and "puttees"—leather, gaiter-like articles that buckled around the leg from the ankle to knee. One warden recalls that these were apt to chafe the ankles, unless worn with high-topped shoes. This was pretty much a dress uniform, and wardens—especially in the backcountry—usually still wore civilian clothes and carried the badge. During the 1940s, the riding britches were replaced with regular trousers that bloused over the tops of ordinary boots. These, along with an Eisenhower-type jacket, made for a more practical uniform.

By 1960, the number of wardens had increased to well over a hundred. Each man was now issued a great variety of equipment from a Warden Service storehouse in Augusta. This was a far cry from a few short years before, when, as one warden recalls, "I got a badge, one law book, and a crinkled road map showing my district outlined with a pencil." Most wardens were now operating state-owned vehicles, and by the early 1960s, everyone was. The two-way radio had been around for a few years in state police vehicles, and they proved to be very worthwhile for game wardens, as well. Retired supervisor Arthur Rogers of Waterville had the first two-way radio in the Warden Service, given to him by the Arnold Trail Fish and Game Club. The first radios were not very powerful, he recalls, and you had to get up on a hill to talk to anyone. Gradually, as money allowed, all vehicles were radio-equipped.

By 1965, the Maine Warden Service was recognized as the best-trained and -equipped organization of its type in the country. Several agencies requested information from time to time as to how our system was designed to operate. On one occasion, information of this nature was sought by a European country that was in the early stages of organizing a warden service.

In 1962, a new job category became important in the Maine Warden Service. Prior to that time, warden supervisors had run their respective divisions single-handedly. Although the position of inspector had been around for several years, it had only been filled once. In 1951, Warden Maynard Marsh was appointed to that position to investigate hunting accidents on a regular basis. (These accidents, by the way, were very numerous in those days. In two years, 1950 and 1952, there were nineteen hunting fatalities per year.) In

1962, to assist the supervisors, ten men were promoted to the rank of inspector. The new job also entailed assisting the district men when problems arose.

It was also during these years that new aspects of the warden's job were being added. When Maine boating law was put into effect, wardens were charged with enforcing this law in regard to registration, operation, and required safety equipment.

When snowmobiles became popular, they, too, were required to be registered and to comply with laws regarding operation. Again, the wardens were designated to enforce these regulations. From time to time, new responsibilities were taken on— enforcing environmental laws, for example. Wardens always seem to rise to the occasion when need be, but understandably may not always accept these new roles with the same degree of enthusiasm as they might in performing their primary function as fish and game law enforcement officers.

In addition to these laws, many new laws were being passed that were extremely beneficial to fish and game conservation. One of the most serious problems encountered by wardens traditionally is that of dogs chasing deer. At times of the year when snow conditions are right, deer become extremely vulnerable to dog predation. Wardens had for years been empowered to shoot dogs found chasing or killing deer, but no laws of a preventive nature existed. Finally, in 1955, as a result of the efforts of Supervisor Maynard Marsh and Superior Court Judge Sullivan, a law was passed that made it illegal for dogs to be in an area frequented by deer. This was but the first step in a series of laws that ultimately resulted in Maine's present statewide leash law. Although the problem of dogs chasing deer will never be completely eliminated, these laws were, and are, a boon to combating the problem.

Soon there were other developments to benefit game wardens in their enforcement work. Two of these had to do with identifying types of meat and establishing the time of death of a deer. Many times a warden will come up with a quantity of meat from some source—usually from a freezer or refrigerator. As you well know, an opinion counts very little in the courtroom, unless perchance it is that of the judge. What the wardens lacked was a foolproof method of identifying various types of wild meat, along with the ability to prove whether it had been previously frozen or not.

Professor David C. O'Meara at the University of Maine had conducted research on this subject and worked out the initial process. Warden Bryan Buchanan became interested in the project, and was given permission to work with O'Meara. Eventually, they finalized a technique that could be utilized and presented to courts as evidence. Laboratory equipment was purchased, and Bryan's expertise became much sought after. His credentials were accepted in several states throughout the Northeast, as well as in one Canadian province, and as the word spread, he eventually spent much time traveling to these places to offer testimony. He also was acknowledged by the federal courts in Massachusetts and Maine as an expert witness in his field.

Developed along similar lines was a process of establishing how long a particular deer had been dead. You may well wonder why this could be of great importance to a warden. Suppose someone were to show up with a deer at a tagging station at eight a.m. He tells you he shot the deer just after daylight, yet it is obvious to you that the deer has been dead considerably longer. We already know about opinions and what they amount to: No proof—no case.

Again, David O'Meara, along with John Gill, did some experimenting. The first of their tests involved postmortem observations on the eyes—that is, significant eye changes following death. Further experiments were performed to record the cooling rates in various parts of a deer's body. These test deer had a known weight and actual time of death. After a long period of study and experimentation, a system based on measuring several factors, including the rate of rigor mortis advancement, was established. Subsequently, several court cases were presented, based on the results, and several wardens were trained in the procedure and received court-accepted certification. This area is constantly undergoing research nationwide in hopes of improving the techniques. However, in the field of meat identification, Bryan Buchanan and David O'Meara were the first to develop it to the point of court acceptance.

Perhaps the most unique change in recent years in the Warden Service's approach to dealing with illegal activities is the use of canines. Canines are used by many law enforcement agencies throughout the country. In situations dealing with fish or game, they really do an outstanding job.

Before a dog may be utilized and his actions accepted by the various courts, he must have some pretty impressive credentials. This goes for the handler as well. In 1980, Sergeant Bill Allen and Warden Deborah Palman became our first wardens to enter this field. Their two German shepherds underwent several months of training at Jerry Sukeforth's facility in Warren, after which, in 1981, both animals underwent a lengthy, rigorous testing program. Upon completion, they were certified by the United States Police Canine Association and ready to go to work. The dogs' training covers a variety of aspects, including protection of the handler, apprehension of violators, tracking of lost or missing people, evidence recovery, and location of fish or game. Within a short time, wardens Jim Ross and Bill Hanrahan acquired dogs, and they also became certified. These animals have added a new dimension to warden work, and have established a worthy record. Several times, their expert noses have tracked down illegally taken game, and more than one fleeing night hunter was hidden, only to suddenly feel a cold nose stuck in his ear. In the dark, this quickly has the desired effect; most fugitives then only wish to surrender.

I am sure by now the reader may realize that I like to give (or at least try to give) credit where it is due. There have undoubtedly been many more significant contributions to the development of the Maine Warden Service over the years. Many of these came, I suspect, from mere suggestions to the right person at the right time, and the true originator will never be known. Twenty years from now, when someone looks back, it may appear that at this present stage we were still in the dark ages of fish and game law enforcement. Still, there is no denying that we have come a long way since 1880.

2 — Warden School

Once the responsibilities of the Warden Service were outlined, the next step was obviously to create a training program so that Maine wardens statewide would follow the same guidelines, and this, too, reflects a major change.

Prior to 1931, wardens had been politically appointed for terms, the length of which changed several times, but were usually for three years' duration. Most wardens were excellent woodsmen, trappers, guides, etc., but some were lacking in other skills, such as being able to read and write. This changed in 1931, when warden candidates first were required to take a Civil Service exam. With more emphasis now on court acceptance and other legal matters, men had to be more than just good woodsmen. Laws protecting fish and game had increased greatly in number since 1890.

The first warden training school was at the University of Maine in 1934, with about one hundred men in attendance. Apparently just getting there was a major problem for some wardens. Leon Wilson, warden at Nine Mile Bridge, remembers it as a three-day trip: "First I hitched a ride on a truck from Nine Mile to Lac-Frontière. Then I went by train to Québec City, where I changed trains and went to Sherbrooke on the Québec Central.

From here, I changed trains again and came down to Holeb on the Canadian Pacific. Someone picked me up and took me to Orono."

Warden school became an annual program, and was moved eventually to Camp Keyes in Augusta. The instructors, for the most part, were wardens themselves, with the older wardens handing down the expertise they had acquired over the years to the younger men. Retired supervisor Raymond Morse from Ellsworth ran the school for nineteen years, and from what I can learn, did an outstanding job. Other agencies frequently enrolled personnel in the Maine Warden School (and still do). Vermont sent people for several years. When Baxter State Park's rangers were commissioned to enforce fish and game laws within the park, they also attended from time to time.

The length of the training session has varied some since the school's inception, but the quality has always improved. At Camp Keyes, the school was conducted for two weeks each year. In the mid-1960s, it was moved back to the University of Maine at Orono, and went for ten weeks. During those years, many of the subjects were taught by professors, and included plant identification, public speaking, and report writing. (I shudder when I think of the reactions of several professors who had never before been exposed to the likes of us.)

For the past few years, near the end of the school in early spring, the class has moved to Swan Island, in the Kennebec River. It is here that the recruits learn techniques from a practical standpoint. Exercises are set up, and wardens go afield and look for violations, as well as violators. This is designed to bring into play their alertness and ability to detect different violations, including illegal traps. Trials are held and evidence presented to simulate legal and courtroom procedure. It is a good learning experience, and is very beneficial in that it puts some pressure on greenhorns to see how they will react in different situations.

In 1983, the warden school was conducted for the first time at the Maine Criminal Justice Academy in Waterville. We now have involved in the school some top-caliber people who have received instruction ratings, as well as a full-time training officer who organizes the sessions. It is indeed a school to be proud of, and we are most fortunate to have it. A surprising number of wardens in Maine these days are college graduates, with degrees ranging from forestry to wildlife management. This is in some contrast to the results of one of the quizzes Raymond Morse gave his class in the early days: One of his questions, he told me, asked each student to write down the different counties in Maine and the dates of the deer season in his own county. One chap did not know any counties except the one he was from! Amazing.

3 — Night Hunters and Falls

I wish I could separate the two elements of this chapter, but they go together hand in hand—night hunters and falls, two of a warden's most frequent measures of endurance.

Game wardens, it seems, are characterized by an ingrained desire to apprehend someone killing, or attempting to kill, a deer at night. Hours upon hours are expended each season in this pursuit. I cannot explain why night hunting seems so horribly wrong to us or why we work so many hours to apprehend perpetrators—we just do.

I have always suspected that it is the excitement involved in snagging a night hunter. You may have been sitting in your vehicle for the prior four hours watching the Big Dipper rotate around the North Star, which really is not all that spectacular. Then, all of a sudden, an old vehicle with a loud muffler or flapping fender (or so it always seems) comes along. Its brake lights come on, and so does your adrenaline switch. Within the next two minutes you may be standing peacefully beside this car advising someone of his rights under Miranda—or going down the road at 90 miles per hour in pursuit of a vehicle that is leaving a trail of lights, guns, and ammunition hurled out the window, or running full-bore across some field after someone who probably has a weapon. Most of the time, however, the vehicle just continues on, and you settle back and say, "Damn, no guts. If he had, he'd have looked in that field."

Occasionally, though, the real thing comes along. I would like to tell you what the real thing is like from the standpoint of several wardens, including myself.

Game wardens usually measure their careers in terms of hunting seasons—that is, falls. One might say to another, "I've worked sixteen falls." Each long fall is a milestone in a warden's career, and for good reason. The strain can be terrible. First of all, you have a working partner with whom you spend night after night after night. Usually, before the night is over, he starts to tell you something you have heard a dozen times before; maybe it's only once, but it seems like more. Your nerves are shot from lack of sleep, and you realize this, so you keep still. Finally, he is all done, and it is quiet at last. Then he digs around in some paper and pulls out some old pistachio nuts. Your car already looks like the bottom of a squirrel's cage. You say nothing, and get out for a stretch and a smoke. (Your partner has sinus trouble, so you do not want to bother him.) You both take a short walk, then come back to the car and get in. It has gotten cold, so you start the car. Now it's warm, and something smells mighty bad. You turn on the flashlight and look at your boots. You now know *exactly* where your partner went for his little walk. Without a word, you pull out and head for home.

This may sound a bit extreme, but I can tell you, it is not. The point is to show how tired, even punchy, you can get. This same guy is maybe the one who taught you how to be a game warden, and who has pulled your fat out of the fire more than once in a tight situation. But you cannot help it. The long fall takes its toll on your nerves, and the lack of a good night's sleep in weeks makes everyone irritable. Long before the season is over, you pray for snow so that the deer will stay put and you can get some rest.

By the way, it is amazing, the things you can see while driving home exhausted at three a.m. Carter Smith tells me he always sees spiders the size of washtubs in the road. Other people see different things. I always have the feeling I am hemmed in by high mountain cliffs on each side of the road. The feeling of disorientation is hard to describe, but Clyde Noyes, now retired, put it to me best, I think: He and Chuck Bessey were watching a field one night, both trying to stave off the clutches of Morpheus. Clyde, whose head was nodding, noticed a vehicle approaching them. "Chuck," he said, "here comes a vehicle." "Yeah," Chuck mumbled. The next time Clyde looked up, the vehicle was just going out of sight. "Chuck, did they light?" he asked. Chuck mumbled, "They haven't got here yet, have they?"

This is where the dedication I have mentioned before comes in. Men in this condition obviously should be home sleeping, but for some reason will just keep plugging, hoping to catch someone with their hand—hopefully their arm—in the jar, so to speak.

There have been some mighty hair-raising episodes involving wardens and night hunters. A few wardens have found themselves playing this midnight cat-and-mouse game with inches and seconds separating life and death.

About the time I went to work as a warden in 1963, another warden, Bryan Buchanan, was pursuing a foot-jacker, when—in Bryan's words—"I heard him cock the gun when he stopped, and I knew he was going to fire at me. I instinctively held my flashlight away from me." He fired, and missed, but not by much. The wadding struck Bryan's arm, and one buckshot pellet hit his flashlight. He apprehended the subject, all right, but I can tell you—when my first chance to chase a foot–hunter arrived, I had that incident on my mind.

The chance came shortly afterward in Washington County, where I was stationed. My man had just gotten out of a vehicle, walked down across a field, and fired a shotgun at a deer. He missed the deer. The flashlight went out, and we assumed he and his partner were going back to the vehicle. Warden Leonard Ritchie and I ran quickly toward the vehicle, hoping to intercept them there, but the vehicle was already moving. As I ran by a large lilac bush at the front of an old farmhouse, I heard a man's legs swishing in the tall grass as he ran. I stopped and cut hard left around the bush, and observed the subject running away across the field. It was a heavy, overcast night, with enough of a moon for some visibility.

About the time I hit full speed, something hit me under the nose, and my feet kept going. My immediate impression was, "Maybe it's like lightning when you are shot—you don't hear the gun." I went down hard. When I got up, I could still make out my assailant. Deciding he had thrown something at me, I took off after him again. As we reached the woods, I was nearly upon him when he suddenly whirled, shone his light in my eyes, and began lunging and screaming and jabbing at me with the light. I had lost my light in the great crash. I knew he had a gun, and not wanting to get shot, I grabbed him, although I was still somewhat blinded by the light.

At this point, he began to whack me on the head with the light. (On a scale of 1 to 10, in terms of pain, I rank this sort of treatment at about an 8.) He got in several good licks as I sort of slipped down. When I got to his knees, I up-ended him, and that was that.

His excuse to the judge was that he thought I was a bear that had jumped on him out of an apple tree. The judge, in turn, asked him if it was common in Washington County for a bear to suddenly appear wearing a red coat immediately after you had fired at a deer at night. The great crash, by the way, and the cut lip were caused by an old wire clothesline strung between two apple trees. The gashes on the head and all those pretty little purple stars were made with the flashlight. The man who performed my baptismal initiation into the Warden Service subsequently went on a five-month vacation in the Machias jail.

There have been many episodes like this over the years, and why someone has not been shot, I will never understand. Several wardens have been shot at by night hunters, luckily without injury. In Charlie Merrill's and Doug Tibbett's case, the subject leaned out of the pursued vehicle and fired twice with a .30-06, striking the door handle on their vehicle.

Sherwood Howes and Amos Steen were pursuing a foot-jacker when he turned and fired at Sherwood. "I felt the bullet go by my face, so I dropped, expecting another. Amos tackled the guy, thinking I had been shot, and he was not being too gentle when I showed up and vigorously began to help. We secured the subject and finally got him to the jail."

Leonard Ritchie's moment of truth came one evening while pursuing a night hunter on foot. This individual had a loaded gun, and from time to time would stop to get his wind and hold Leonard at bay with the gun. He finally turned to run again, ran face-first into a large rock, and was captured.

Obviously, not all cases fall into the "deadly" category. Some take outrageously funny twists, but nevertheless, the potential for extreme danger is always present in a night-hunting situation. It all depends on the type of persons involved and what they do when the warden appears. Most night hunters, at least in my experience, are terrified of being caught, and sometimes a terrified person will react in a way that is completely different from his usual nature. Anyone whom I have ever caught at night on foot has turned with the gun when spoken to. You had sure better have your eyes open; he might fire from fright, not really meaning to.

As for the humorous aspects of many night-hunting episodes—it is entirely likely that whether or not something is funny depends on which side you are on. Take, for instance, the night Dan Watson, Roger Wolverton, and myself pursued a pickup truck at a high rate of speed down a winding gravel road. Suddenly, the passenger door opened and a flashlight rolled out. At this point, the vehicle sort of lurched into the ditch. The passenger fled from the vehicle clutching a rifle, and ran into the woods with Roger on his heels.

Shortly thereafter, Roger appeared with the subject, but no rifle. A brief search produced the gun. The man had run into a fir tree about head high and bent it over, whereupon it flung him backward into Roger's grasp. While using my light to gather up some cartridges that had rolled out when the man ran, I noticed that the right front tire was flat. I made a remark to the effect of, "Gee, it isn't every day the vehicle you're pursuing has a flat tire and has to stop." With his head hung, the fellow said, "I ain't sure, but I think that gun might have had something to do with that tire." He was right. I pulled the floor mat down, and there was a neat, round little hole in the floor. In the haste of jacking the shells out of that old lever-action, he had shot the tire off.

My friend Norman Moulton always talks about the Great Game Warden in the Sky who's looking out for us. I guess, all in all, he does a pretty good job.

One night, Sherwood Howes found some night hunters killing a deer in his dooryard, and that is where they got caught.

On more than one occasion, night hunters in a vehicle have dropped off one of their cronies after killing a deer, then driven off, the idea being to pick up him and the deer in a few minutes. Sometimes, if this works out right, the vehicle is stopped some distance away, and the warden comes back instead. This is a great trick, if you can pull it off.

Sherwood Howes talks of the night he and Amos Steen overheard some night hunters making plans in their stopped car. The driver told the subject who got out that he would pick him up later at the top of the hill. The wardens stopped the car down the road, and Sherwood got in. In a few minutes, he instructed the driver to go to the top of the hill and stop. When they got to the top of the hill and stopped, another car happened to be coming from some distance away. The man appeared, opened the door, and said excitedly, "Let me in, for Christ's sake. The wardens are coming." Sherwood grabbed him by the coat and said, "Get right in!"

There appear to be at least two kinds of night hunters. One is the incidental hunter, who shoots the deer that steps into the road on his way home from a hunting trip; the other is the deliberate night-jacker. It is the second type of hunter we spend so many hours on. Many night–hunted deer traditionally have been sold to nonresident hunters. Market hunting and night hunting go hand in hand, and this has always been a problem for wardens. Selling deer can be good business, provided the hunter screens his customers thoroughly. Many do not screen well enough, though, and this has given the Warden Service a really effective way of dealing with the problem.

It is amazing, the extent to which people have gone to kill

deer at night. The variety of techniques attempted is very wide indeed. Using snares is a particularly deadly method. One technique used along the Québec boundary years ago involved felling a tree across a deer path in a yard and for several nights letting them get used to jumping over it. Then, a file ground to a point with a razor edge was driven into the tree at an upward angle. The next time a deer jumped over the tree, it was all over.

Night hunters have been apprehended with crossbows and longbows, as well. One crossbow seized had a bow made from a ground-down car spring. Warden John Ford once apprehended some subjects in a camp who had set out to net a deer. A net had been suspended over some apples, and the triggering device was connected to a line that ran to the camp. When a deer tripped the mechanism, the net fell, and a can in the camp dumped some rocks into the sink, alerting the occupants to come out and check the net—and in this case, to meet the wardens.

Of all these devices implemented by night hunters, it is without a doubt a set gun and the possibility of stumbling into it that causes us the most concern. I have never seen one in place, but once saw where one had once been. The typical set gun is nothing more than an old single-barreled shotgun tied next to a deer path with a trip string. In a gun dealer's collection, though, I once saw a gun that was held in position by a long spike that was pushed into the ground. A swivel device allowed the gun to swing and elevate in the direction of whatever was tripping it. It was a hideous-looking thing, with a short barrel and no hammer. It appeared to be a factory-made device. The firing mechanism was a plunger with a knob that was pulled back to cock the gun. Such an instrument is not something anyone wants to locate the hard way in the dark.

Quite frequently, night hunters have been apprehended in trees. I remember one man, in fact, who shot himself out of a tree when he dropped his shotgun. It struck butt-first in a crotch below him, and went off. He was not too seriously wounded. Good lesson, though, wouldn't you say?

On another occasion, a night hunter in the backseat of a car became excited because he thought he and his buddies were about to be apprehended, and discharged his rifle. The bullet went through the seat and killed the driver.

Luckily, most night hunters do not wish anybody any harm, and after they are caught offer only lies and wild excuses about looking for their dog. Sometimes, however, serious injuries have occurred in night–hunting incidents. High-speed chases happen quite frequently, and wardens dread this line of duty most of all. The idea of a $500 fine and three days in jail is not that appealing to most offenders; the urge to get away is strong. Most of Maine's roads are not engineered for high-speed chases at night. Many times, the perpetrator loses control of his vehicle on a corner and winds up in a wreck. Game wardens are not immune, by any means, and more than one has wound up climbing out of a window in disgust. Then comes that painful call to the supervisor to tell him the good news.

One time, I remember, a vehicle had arrived at the field where I was waiting, but when I went to start my cruiser, the battery was dead. Now, you talk about a painful lesson! Getting stuck or hung up on a rock in the middle of a field when the vehicle you have been waiting for is slowly approaching with a light out the window is another sad occasion. You see now that the Great Game Warden in the Sky is not always watching.

During the 1940s and '50s, deer were very plentiful. It is

during such times that night hunting is very widespread. In those years, several wardens received serious injuries attempting to apprehend night hunters. Two wardens, Irwin Bonney and Maynard Marsh, were run over deliberately by vehicles, and their legs were terribly mangled. Both recovered from their injuries, but their legs were never quite the same again.

Another interesting segment of history specific to night hunters is the construction of Maine's Interstate 95. In the late 1960s, I-95 was extended north from Howland, through one of the best deer territories in Maine—Mattamiscontis. The sides of the road were seeded with clover, and soon deer stood along the break-down lanes for miles on both sides, just tempting potential night hunters. Unfortunately, many of them yielded to temptation. Even the interstate troopers got involved in the fracas. (It broke up the monotony on the night shift, I suppose.) Several troopers caught night hunters, and did an excellent job of it. Our whole warden division spent most of one fall out there, and by the end had appre-hended sixty-five night hunters. It was a cat-and-mouse game played to the extreme. This road was made for high-speed chases, and many did occur.

Several humorous incidents occurred on I-95, but one is unique. Wardens Bob Smith and Clyde Speed were observing two approaching vehicles, which then stopped approximately one and a half miles away. One swung around, proceeded north a short way, then swung again and stopped behind the first vehicle. Sometimes you cannot hear a shot, so when the vehicles proceeded, south-bound, the wardens stopped them both. The large van and the dump truck contained five hunters from Connecticut who had been to Newfoundland on a moose hunt. In the van were two moose, cut up and iced down; the hunters possessed valid permits for these. However, in the back of the truck was a spike-horned buck that was very warm. All five men were arrested, and a trooper showed up to assist the wardens. At this point, the boys dug into their duffel and all wanted pictures of each other posing with the officers, with the cruisers' blue lights flashing. No problem.

Off they went to the jail in Lincoln, where they were to post bail. Once there, the leader of the group checked with the others to see how much money each had, and how much each fellow needed to make up the $200 cash bail. He wrote it down to keep track, then pulled a roll of bills from his pocket that would choke a horse. After counting off ten $100 bills, he laughed and said, "I told you guys to bring a lot of money." At this point, they were told they were free to go. "You mean, we don't have to go to jail?" "No, you don't. You're free to go," Bob said. "Now wait a minute," said the man. "For $1,000, it seems like we ought to be able to say we were put in jail." The turnkey agreed, and out they went to the vehicles to get their cameras. After taking pictures of one another through the bars, they drove off. They also left enough money for five copies of the next edition of the Lincoln paper to be mailed to them. Night hunters—from one extreme to the other, you never know what this unpredictable breed will do.

4 — THE BOUNDARY

For some reason, the boundary line between two nations tends to attract trouble—if not geographical, then economical. In our own case, the differences have usually been over fish and game.

The Maine-Québec border is unique. In some places it is fairly straight; in others, it is quite convoluted. We also have a Maine–New Brunswick border; but when a warden says "the boundary," he usually is referring to Québec, and with good reason. If you look at a map, you'll notice that just west of the Maine-Québec boundary, there are roads and small towns everywhere. Terrain features change pretty much at the boundary, in that the Canadian towns, farms, fields, and roads just sort of stop—and from there, eastward into Maine, it is all forest for miles. For these Canadians, the border country has always been more or less their backyard when it comes time to hunt or fish.

As I mentioned earlier, fish and game problems arose early in this region. Due to its remoteness (from our side), any enforcement attempt was at first nearly impossible due to lack of roads and wardens to patrol. Eventually, as the Maine Warden Service developed, wardens were stationed along the boundary, in the early log camps built for housing—two wardens to a camp, due to the risk as well as the remoteness factor. A man alone was in a very precarious position, injury or sickness being just two of the hazards. There were hundreds of Canadian woodsmen in the lumber camps, and wardens snowshoed miles and miles each winter, watching for snares—a favorite Canadian method of taking animals illegally. In the event that someone was apprehended, it was quite likely that a warden's problems had only just begun.

Eben Perry recalls an incident that occurred on the Northwest Branch of the St. John River. He had located an illegal bear trap a short way from the river. After he had spent two nights and three days watching it, the trapper, a Canadian, showed up to tend it. The trapper had a rifle, which he pointed at Eben, and a scuffle ensued. Finally, Eben loaded the trapper into the canoe, and they started downriver. At this point, the man was wearing the bear-trap chain around his neck to discourage him from jumping out.

But the lack of sleep had taken its toll on Eben, and he had to catch a wink, so they put into a camp along the river for the night. To secure his prisoner, Eben put the trapper's clothes into a bedding box and nailed it shut; then he handcuffed the chap to the bedspring, and went to sleep. The following morning, a warden plane picked them up and took them to Fort Kent. Once they were airborne, the Canadian—who obviously had never been in a plane before—poked Eben, looked out his window, and pointed down. With a grin, he said in French, "Not worry, I not jump now."

Most wardens who were here, especially in the early days, have similar stories of trying to bring a prisoner downriver to Fort Kent, covering sometimes a distance of ninety miles in a canoe.

It was a three-day trip sometimes to get back upriver to Nine Mile Bridge, recalls Leon Wilson. By vehicle, it was a 240-mile trip over rough roads. Facilities were sometimes primitive at best in the warden camps. Leon Wilson recalls arriving at the Nine Mile Bridge warden camp in December 1932, after hitching a ride on a truck from Lac Frontiere. The warden before him had died, and the camp had been vacant for some time. Canadian woodsmen had been using it as a stopover on the way back and forth from Clayton Lake and Lac Frontiere. Most of the poles that had served as the floor had been pulled up and burned in the stove. The windows were all smashed; there was no furniture. Leon says, "I damn near turned around and went home right then. But by June, when my wife and two kids came to live with me, I had made some furniture— including a mattress woven of strips from cut-up tires. We were there seven years before we were transferred."

Leon, by the way, has the distinction of being mentioned in more books than any other warden I know of. These include *Nine Mile Bridge* by Helen Hamlin, wife of Warden Curly Hamlin; *My Life in the Maine Woods* by Annette Jackson, wife of Warden Dave Jackson; and two books by Louise Dickinson Rich, *We Took to the Woods* and *My Neck of the Woods*.

Several strange occurrences involving wardens along the Boundary have taken place over the years. The following incident still remains a mystery to this day.

On November 11, 1922, Divisional Chief Warden Dave Brown from Greenville and one of his wardens, young Mertley Johnson from Patten, headed north from Greenville. Johnson had been assigned by his chief to look into some beaver-poaching in the area west of Chesuncook Lake and north of Moosehead Lake. (This was an annual problem in those days. Game wardens spent much of their time in that country patrolling the area between

Mount Katahdin and the Québec boundary for illegal Canadian trapping.) It was common knowledge that a ring of Canadians had made remarks and threats directed at any wardens who might try to interfere. What Johnson told Brown when he arrived in Greenville is not known, but they both headed north carrying packs and weapons; Brown had a Winchester rifle, and Johnson, a revolver in a leg holster. Brown told his family they would return by Thanksgiving.

Thanksgiving came and went, and still no word had been received from the two wardens. As anxiety turned to fear, Deputy Sheriff Adelbert Rogers, a longtime friend of Brown, began an investigation, and a band of wardens and veteran woodsmen began to pick up a rather cold trail. Men at the Great Northern Paper Company camp at Loon Stream had seen the two wardens late in the afternoon of November 14. According to the men, the wardens had been in good spirits and well equipped to stay out if they had to. They had spent the night at Loon Stream Camp, but had said very little about their mission. Somehow, though, it was generally understood by these men that the wardens intended to go to Abacotnetic Bog on the headwaters of the North Branch of the St. John River, then to Chamberlain Lake and home.

The next evidence of them was at Half-Way Camp, operated by Arthur De Roche on the North Branch of the Penobscot River. On November 15, the wardens had eaten a lunch prepared by the camp cook, Mrs. Drolet, who worked for Mr. De Roche. Brown and Johnson had told Mr. and Mrs. Drolet that they intended to go on to Big Bog Dam and spend the night at a shelter called Kennedy's.

Deputy Rogers was able to find what he knew to be trail signs made by his friend Dave Brown. These signs had turned eastward and gone up Big Brook, away from Big Dam. At some point along Big Brook, the group came to a beaver house that appeared to have been set up (trapped) during the previous closed season. It was here that it first appeared to the searchers that Brown and Johnson were on to something hot, so to speak. Continuing on, the group came to a survey crew who stated they had seen the men and given them a couple of boxes of raisins.

Pushing on, the men found on the shore a small evergreen shelter. It was hidden from view by anyone coming along the trail, to or from the beaver house where the traps had been. The trail ended here with the two empty raisin boxes. The two wardens had disappeared on the night of November 15.

Word spread rapidly about the missing wardens. All camps were checked, and everyone in the country who could be reached was questioned—to no avail. Many theories were brought up, but none seemed valid. The most reasonable one was that the men had tried to cross Big Bog on thin ice and had drowned. Snow had covered the ground since their disappearance, and ice had formed. Yet Big Bog, although large in area, was relatively shallow, and it did not seem likely that both men had drowned. It was known that Dave Brown was a non-swimmer, but Mert Johnson was a strong swimmer. To complicate matters, investigation showed that Big Bog had not been frozen over on November 15.

Clues drifted in. One subject from Saint-Zacharie stated that he had heard what sounded like two rifle shots in that area on the day in question. This man said that he had been working at Half-Way Camp for De Roche and had been tending some traps on the North Branch that day, and had heard the two shots while returning to camp. It was deer season, so it was possible that he had heard deer hunters, but no evidence was found to support this. A search of the area turned up a .22-caliber rifle hidden in the woods. The man from Saint-Zacharie admitted it was his, and that he kept it hidden so he would not get into trouble with the wardens.

A primitive woods-telephone line ran between several of the camps in the area, and at some point it was discovered that two Canadian cousins who were at the Forty Mile Camp had received a mysterious phone call on the night of November 14. Other men in the camp stated that, in their opinion, the call had been to warn them that game wardens were in the area. After the call, one of the two appeared afraid; the other had seemed angry and defiant. They had left camp, supposedly to check their traps.

The attempt to locate and question these men began immediately. Eventually, a farmer from Québec was located, and he reluctantly told the authorities what he knew. On November 16, he had given a ride back to Canada to one of the two cousins—a man known to the Canadian authorities as a surly, bad-tempered customer who had been in trouble with the law previously. The farmer was afraid to talk, but was persuaded to relate his story. He told authorities that the man told him he had been hunting deer across the border and had shot two deer. When the farmer asked him why he didn't have any meat with him, the man said, "It wasn't that kind of deer, but it was the best day's work I ever did." The farmer also remembered that he made some mention of not being easily scared off.

When arriving at the home of the other cousin in Canada, Sheriff Rogers found him very scared and reluctant to say anything that would anger the man in question. He finally did admit that they had been across the boundary, hunting and trapping in Maine, and had returned home frightened when they heard wardens were in the area.

When finally questioned by the sheriff and a translator, the suspect refused to answer questions and ordered the authorities out of the house. Rumors that the two wardens had been murdered were very prevalent in Saint-Zacharie and Saint-Prosper.

Deputy Rogers again confronted the suspect in his family's store and explained to him his theory that he had shot the two wardens, then carried them to the water and thrown them in. No proof existed, and the suspect denied the accusations.

At this point, the deputy returned to the residence of the first cousin, who was married to the suspect's sister, and informed her that Maine authorities had offered a $2,000 reward for information as to the wardens' whereabouts, dead or alive.

Shortly thereafter, the sister of the suspect arrived at Big Bog, where two warden members of the investigation party had been stationed for the winter. She stated that in a dream she had seen a vision that had shown her the location of the wardens' bodies. She led authorities to the shore, and indicated where the bodies would be found under the ice. When a search yielded nothing, she left, very angry at not being able to claim the reward. This convinced authorities even more that foul play was involved, but still no proof existed.

After a long winter, wardens Sandy Mullen and Bert Duty found Johnson's body in early May, washed up against Big Bog Dam. It had been brought down by high water. Johnson's holster was unsnapped and his revolver missing. The two packs belonging to the men were located later the same day. Dave Brown's body was found on May 3, about a mile below the dam, hung up in some brush .

The news of the grim discovery was carried by Mullen, who traveled from Big Bog Dam over slush-covered trails and swollen streams to a telephone at Loon Stream, 38 miles away and back, in an unbelievable six hours and fifteen minutes.

Then began the arduous task of bringing the bodies to civilization. Because of existing conditions, this in itself was a tremendous job. The last stage was completed by canoe. It was obvious that the bodies had been in the water for a long period. The men's watches had stopped within two minutes of each other.

Dave Brown's rifle was never found, but rumors were heard from time to time of a rifle matching its description that had been seen in Canada. John Brown, Dave's brother, went to Canada, but was never able to locate the rifle.

Forensic techniques so common today in crime investigations were not developed to their present level back then, and although autopsies were performed, nothing conclusive was ever established as the cause of death of either man. The prime suspect reportedly left his hometown shortly afterward and was not seen again. This case remained unsolved; now, more than sixty years later, it most assuredly always will.

I am extremely indebted to David Brown's daughter-in-law, Ina Ladd Brown, for the information connected with this event. She wrote a magazine article many years ago concerning the disappearance of her father-in-law and Mertley Johnson.

Without a doubt, this was the most outstanding incident involving wardens along the boundary. There have been others that could have been as tragic. Every boundary warden, with few exceptions, has had a gun held on him at one point or another. Several wardens have been shot at, and many have had close calls involving wrestling a gun away from someone, then subduing the subject and taking him into custody.

Warden Phil Dumond at Estcourt Station once apprehended two subjects with a deer on a skidder, and escorted them to their camp, supposedly to obtain cash bond money. Upon entering the camp, one of the men grabbed a rifle from behind the door, stuck it in Phil's face, and asked if he was afraid. Phil told him to put the gun down and to stop the foolishness. At this point, the gun went off. This had a startling effect on the man, and he put the gun down without further resistance. When Dumond finally arrived home and went to wash up, he noticed that his face was black on one side from powder burns. A very close call, to say the least!

Québec has had a moose season for many years. The boundary is a popular spot, since most of the moose live in Maine, not Québec. Hunters flock to the border area, sometimes building treestands, and call moose from the Maine side onto the boundary, which is merely a swath cut through the woods. It is permissible to shoot a moose if it is on the boundary.

The problem is that quite frequently, the hunters intrude onto the Maine side. Some Canadians have made elaborate attempts to hide equipment such as snowmobiles, tents, and food deep into Maine weeks prior to the season, and wardens will walk miles and miles of the border, looking for telltale signs of illegal crossing. Many of these poachers are very clever at concealing their comings and goings, and it takes a skilled person to detect it.

One such operation was located weeks before the season opened. When the season arrived, wardens worked shifts, keeping the concealed base camp under surveillance. It was located many miles from any kind of road access, and getting there required a considerable hike. Finally, the poachers came to the campsite. The tent was pitched, and the hunt begun. Many hours later, in the dark and pouring rain, the wet and cold, the wardens closed in around the camp and made the apprehension. Laughing, dry faces inside the tent suddenly turned very glum indeed.

It has always been traditional for wardens along the bound-

ary, because they deal primarily with Canadians, to seize equipment of some sort to assure the return of the subject arrested. Most
of the Canadians involved are employed in the woods, and their
only possession of any significant value is a chain saw. Warden Eben
Perry (now retired) worked the boundary for several falls. His
garage contained so many seized saws that the local citizenry, what
there was of it, referred to him as "Judge Homelite."

Ever since wardens began to patrol the boundary and its districts,
this has been the area where new wardens are sent for their break-
in periods. When snowshoes were the only way in, it took young
men with the eagerness and stamina to snowshoe hundreds of
miles each winter along the border, keeping an eye out for illegal
activities. Their snowshoe floats served as a warning to those who
might venture across that they might not be alone. (Every spring,
in earlier years, the dozens of sugar camps operated by Canadian
families had to be visited from time to time for the same reason.)
To some, the mere suspicion of a warden's presence is quite often
a deterrent. Since a warden (despite his reputation for mysterious
appearances) can be in only one place at a time, the next best thing
to being ubiquitous is for him to give the impression that he might
be in the area, even if he is not. Then, at some point, he'll reverse
the procedure and see who is doing what.

Most wardens stay only a few years on the boundary, then
move out, usually because of school-aged children. Some, like
Warden Specialist Rod Sirois and his family, enjoy the woods and
have made it their permanent home. They reside in T15 R15
(Township 15, Range 15) at Saint–Pamphile, Québec. The children
attend school in Québec, and are bilingual. You might think this an
odd home for a college graduate with a commercial pilot's license.

An ex–Navy Seal, Rod might seem out of place here, but I can assure you, he is not. One of his experiences as a warden involved wrestling with a very formidable foe who was trying his best to do him in with a gun. Wrong thing to do. The subject was subdued after a fashion, then taken into custody.

Several of the camps built by wardens years ago were later replaced with houses or mobile homes in which wardens along the boundary lived for many years. Gradually, as the network of lumber roads extended farther, access to many of these areas became easier. The houses or camps were sold, and wardens began to patrol the areas on a less-regular basis. Only four districts still provide state housing. In addition to Saint–Pamphile, accommodations at only Estcourt Station, Daquaam, and Boundary Cottage now remain.

Warden Phil Dumond has been at Estcourt Station for most of his twenty-eight years as a warden, and I am sure he has no plans to move. Estcourt Station, by the way, is as far up in Maine as you can go. Phil once had the Mount Desert district. It reminded him, he said, of a park with "nothing but bushes and people everywhere." So, ever since, it has been the woods for him, and he has done one hell of a job there for all those years.

The boundary has always been a unique spot for game wardens to work. It may have lost some of its uniqueness in modern times due to increased accessibility, but it is still probably the most challenging area in Maine for a warden.

5 — Lost Persons and Searches

Each and every year, several hundred people disappear in the United States. Most of them eventually turn up, are rescued, or found (dead or alive). Mysteriously, though, between two to three hundred missing persons each year are never seen again. Broken down into groups, they include some who have run away, others who have been abducted, and many who have just plain gotten lost in unfamiliar surroundings. Lost individuals become the responsibility of various agencies throughout the country, depending on which state you live in. In many states, sheriff's departments or state police will search for missing persons. When someone becomes lost in Maine, searching for that person becomes the responsibility of Maine game wardens.

Due to the rural character of much of Maine, we deal with a large number of these incidents each year. During an average year, we respond to somewhat over three hundred calls for assistance in locating lost, missing, or overdue people. Many of these cases are resolved fairly quickly, and are not of a serious nature. The average overdue canoeists are found intact, simply windbound, as we suspected; or the missing fisherman has a conked-out motor, and simply needs a tow.

Sometimes, though, the person does not turn up, and the nature of the situation changes. It is then that the woods knowledge and tracking skills of a warden are sought. I think that the role played by wardens in recovering lost people in Maine is a worthy one, and I'd like to relate some of these stories. A search for someone lost is, most of all, a mystery—and you know how everyone loves a mystery.

The first search to receive a great deal of publicity in Maine was the search for young Donn Fendler, the schoolboy who became lost while climbing Mount Katahdin in 1939. The book about his experiences, Lost on a Mountain in Maine, was required reading for schoolchildren for many years. Donn became separated from his group in the dense fog (clouds) which frequently obliterates the trail markers above the timberline. His determination to live and his coolheadedness enabled him to continue for many days on berries until he came to the East Branch of the Penobscot River. People from a camp across the river spotted him and returned him downriver by canoe to civilization. Many woodsmen, game wardens, fire wardens, state police, and sheriffs were involved in this search. It is likely that the need to decide who should be responsible for directing searches for lost people in Maine arose here.

In 1943, the Legislature passed a law that stated that game wardens would conduct searches for people who became lost in the fields and forests of Maine. It was not, however, until many years later that the Maine Warden Service was actually mandated as the primary agency in regard to actually managing these search efforts.

By sheer coincidence, in 1943, right after the law was passed, wardens became very involved in an episode that has become almost legendary in the North Country. My longtime friend, Helon Taylor, who was a warden supervisor during those days, relates the story.

In June of 1943, a young guide named Wesley Porter from Patten had spent the day moving a party from Matagamon Lake up Webster Stream to a camp on Webster Lake, where they were to spend a few days fishing. Upon his return to the camp with a second load of dunnage, he asked if anyone had moved the canoe in his absence. His sports acknowledged they had not, and he did not mention it again. However, Porter had a good reason for asking: Ever since spring breakup, several camps in the area had been broken into, and food had been stolen. Several camps had had a window or two broken by a shotgun blast.

That evening, as Wes left the shore of the lake to return to the camp, a shot rang out. One pellet struck him under the chin and killed him.

An investigation was begun by state police. A month later, no leads as to the murderer's identity had surfaced.

Helon says, "I had a theory on what had happened, and Commissioner Stobie called me in to Augusta to hear it. I told him that during World War I, many Canadians had hidden out in the woods around Eustis and Chain of Ponds to avoid conscription into the Canadian army. My theory was that this was a similar case—perhaps the murderer was a Canadian draft-dodger who was hiding out and surviving by breaking into camps for food. Stobie told me to take some wardens and bring him out, one way or another. I told him I would like Warden Bert Duty for one of the men; Duty was a friend of mine whom I knew to be an excellent woodsman and tracker.

"Pilot Bill Turgeon landed us at Nugent's Camps on

Chamberlain Lake, but we soon discovered that it, too, had been broken into and food stolen, along with a 20-gauge shotgun. Other camps in the area on Snake Pond, Carpenter Pond, and Hudson Pond had all been broken into, and all shared the shotgun blast through a window. Some of the men were staying at the Soper Mountain fire warden's camp, and some at Clear Lake Camp. One evening, when wardens Bert Duty and Charlie Harriman returned to Clear Lake Camp, they discovered that they had been broken into as well. There were several missing items—food, some cigars, and a coat belonging to Harriman. Harriman was very concerned, and remarked, 'If worst comes to worst, boys, and you have to shoot him, don't shoot him in the body. I don't want any holes in my coat!' "

The search continued. Warden Bert Duty and another searcher were planning to spend the night at the Soper Mountain fire warden's camp. A Great Northern Paper Company forester had observed the subject in this area, and had let him pass by while he remained unobserved. Things were rather tense, to say the least. This subject had proven he was very woods-wise, and had already killed once. Helon advised his men to sleep outside the camp and take turns watching it during the night. They decided to compromise and sleep inside, taking turns staying up with no lamp lit.

Bert took the first watch. Sometime later, he struck a match to have a smoke. He instantly realized his mistake, and made a dive for the floor. It was a lucky move for Bert, for just then a charge of shot came through the window and demolished the phone on the wall. Together under a bunk, the wardens waited for their subject's next move. None came, but I would not have wanted to have been some innocent visitor who came to call on them for the rest of that night.

Search efforts were intensified somewhat at this point. Helon felt that a bloodhound might be a good addition to the team, so a Connecticut state trooper and his hound were flown to the area. The search had gone on for slightly over a month, when suddenly the man was confronted in a swamp by some searchers. When spoken to, he dropped the ax he was carrying and started to swing the shotgun—a fateful mistake, for a member of the party fired, wounding the subject in the leg.

Retired supervisor Sleepy Atkins was a pilot in those days, and was involved in the search. He recalls seeing a man on the shore of Musquacook Lake, waving his arms. "I landed," Sleepy recalls, "thinking he must have some news, and he did. The man told me of the wounding and capture of the suspected murderer. The subject was carried by stretcher to shore, and we flew him to Greenville. His wound would not have generally been considered serious, but he was not in good physical condition due to his months of foraging. He went into shock and died that evening in the hospital. He was, in fact, a Canadian draft–dodger."

In 1944 there were about 350,000 German POWs in the United States. Over 2,000 of these were being held in four POW camps in Maine. These camps were located in Houlton, Princeton, Seboomook Lake, and Spencer Lake. The prisoners were employed as woodcutters and received a small wage per cord. On several occasions escapes were made, and wardens were called to help capture the Germans.

Helon Taylor recalls some of these captures:

"The prisoners at the Spencer Lake camp were cutting wood on a mile square. The only guards were at the corners, so escape could be made fairly easily; the remoteness and the fact that it was winter were the only real deterrents to doing so."

One escape attempt was made by two men who secretly had

been hoarding their noon lunches for provisions. When it was discovered they were missing, Helon was contacted, and, with some
of the best woodsmen in the Warden Service, he began a search.
Deer were plentiful in the area, and it was soon discovered that the
men were traveling along the deer trails and leaving no footprints.
At various points when they wished to change direction, they were
able to go for great distances on the snow's thick crust to another
deer trail, again, leaving very little trace of their passing. Once the
general direction of travel was determined, the trail became easier
to find. Several days later, they were captured without resistance.
They had fashioned snowshoes from boards, and had managed to
go quite far south. Their plan had been, according to them, to with
luck reach the coast, board a neutral vessel, and go to Argentina.

Another group escaped from the Princeton camp, and Helon
and several other wardens were involved in capturing them, with
one amusing incident that Helon remembers: "A search plane
reported having spotted campfire smoke, so we checked our
weapons and proceeded to make the long walk to the specified
area," Helon relates. "We approached the campsite very quietly.
Finally, with guns drawn, we made the rush—and found nothing
but an old lightning-struck stub still smoking. You talk about a
letdown!"

For years, most of the people we searched for were hunters or fishermen. Most were found, but occasionally someone would be to all
effects swallowed up by the woods, with never a trace found. Or, a
skeleton would turn up, usually found by another hunter or
woodsman.

These lost persons who were never found have always provided many hours of conversation around the wardens' camp

stoves. It always starts out, "I wonder what ever happened to old so-and-so."

A case that has always haunted me involved a man from Newry named Fred Kilgore. Fred was a man known by everyone up and down Bear River Valley. In May of 1948, he returned from the woods behind his house where he had been working. After supper, he told his wife he had forgotten his ax and was going after it. He and the dog went to the woods. The dog returned. Fred did not. To this day, that is all anyone knows. A large search was conducted for days, with no clue or reason for his disappearance ever found. I was only a boy at the time, but I can remember the intrigue surrounding Fred's disappearance. I have been involved in similar situations as a warden, helping to conduct searches, and believe me, it is intriguing and frustrating, to say the least.

My first involvement as a warden in an extensive search was an extremely interesting one. One July evening in 1965, I received a call from Baxter Park at my home in Grindstone. (That's right, Grindstone—the mere name helps describe this unique spot on the East Branch of the Penobscot River.) Two boys were missing from Roaring Brook Campground. This was in my partner's, Elmer Knowlton's, district, but they could not contact him, so would I come?

Upon our arrival, Ranger Rodney Sargent and I discovered that the two brothers, Robbie and Tim Mott, ages seventeen and three, had not been seen since afternoon, when campers had seen them walking up and down the campground's access road. We spent the night going up and down along the banks of Roaring Brook, looking for clues. Earlier in the day, the boys had been at Sandy Stream Pond not far from the campsite, so we looked in that area, also.

At dawn, two Maine State Prison bloodhounds arrived. We took them down along the brook, but eventually whatever scent they were on to apparently gave out, and we brought the dogs back. The older brother was mentally retarded and also had diabetes; these factors added a greater degree of urgency to the matter. Very quickly, the effort intensified.

Warden Supervisor Dave Priest was soon directing a search effort unparalleled in Maine at that time. Within two days there were literally hundreds of searchers on the scene. The one-way road in and out of Roaring Brook Campground became clogged at times with vehicles transporting an army of searchers, and enough food and supplies to provide for them. Huge military helicopters were searching and also transporting searchers to more remote areas. Civil Defense feeding units were set up to feed people around the clock. Dozens of wardens, park rangers, and professional foresters were directing groups of searchers in making grid sweeps; others were out establishing baselines for future crews to use on sweeps. National Guard personnel, Air Force personnel, and people from where-all-I-do-not-know showed up to search for the two missing boys. They numbered literally in the hundreds on most days.

The days continued. A week went by; no clues. Searchers were becoming exhausted and were replaced by fresh ones from as far away as New York State. The terrain around Mount Katahdin has never been called gentle—beautiful, perhaps, but not gentle—and a new pair of boots could be worn out in a week. Searchers sprained ankles and received other assorted injuries. The nights were cold, and on several, there was frost. The search had been expanded in all directions and was receiving national media attention by now. Shades of doubt and even suspicion began to grow in some of our minds. Supervisor Dave Priest, however, remained unflappable. He insisted they were here somewhere—we just had not found the spot. We did, however, all agree that by now we were undoubtedly looking for two bodies.

Dave's persistence paid off. He directed searchers to go back and re-search areas that had been searched before. It was in one of these areas that finally, on the tenth day, the bodies of the Mott brothers were found. They were together about one·and·a·half miles from the campsite. Searchers had been very close.

This sad incident was the first truly massive search effort conducted by game wardens. There were to be others, to be sure. Although no serious problems arose, it did serve to bring out the logistical problems that arise in managing a large search. It was some time before we learned to handle these problems more effectively.

Another lost-person incident that is, I think, extremely unique happened in 1974. Augustus Aldrich was not your usual man. He had done many adventurous things in his life, including being the first person to climb the stairs all the way to the top of the Empire State Building. He had spent most of his life climbing mountains. Katahdin was his favorite, and he had made many trips to the area from his home in Vermont. It was no great surprise, then, that he and a woman companion, whom he enthusiastically wanted to see the beauty of Katahdin, showed up at Chimney Pond. What would have to be considered surprising by most standards was that he was eighty-six years old.

The morning after they arrived at Chimney Pond he went to the ranger's cabin, but he returned to his campsite very upset at having found a notice on the bulletin board stating that because of the weather, the trails to the summit were closed for the day. He then disappeared—and I mean disappeared. A weeklong search by dozens of volunteers and search-and-rescue teams failed to turn up a clue.

Again, helicopters were used to ferry searchers and food into Chimney Pond. The terrain around this part of the mountain is very capable of swallowing up a man; there are hundreds of hidden holes under the brush in which a car-sized object could suddenly vanish. It is so rough, in fact, that we regrettably had to send some of the younger volunteers back down for safety reasons. It is very frustrating, I discovered, to not find your man; you wonder if you have done something wrong, somehow. Gus Aldrich is still some-where on Mount Katahdin, and I suspect that there is where he wants to be.

As I mentioned earlier, a certain number of lost persons are never found. Without a doubt, the largest search ever conducted in Maine was, unfortunately, another of these cases.

On Labor Day weekend, 1975, a small boy was reported missing from a campground on Natanis Pond in the Chain of Ponds region north of Eustis. Kurt Newton was three and a half years old when he disappeared. The small tricycle he was riding was found at the campground dump, not too far from the camp-site. Before long, it seemed like all the wardens in Maine were there, and at least half the citizens.

Many law enforcement agencies worked together on this search. At one point, there were approximately 2,000 people involved in the effort to find the boy. The terrain was being scoured so thoroughly that lost personal items like combs and cigarette lighters were being found in the woods a mile away and turned in.

Every resource available was put to the best possible use. A military airplane equipped with a special infrared heat-seeking device was flown from Florida to assist. But the boy was never found.

A large search always takes on several aspects. It can become political, and it usually does. The media people arrive in droves. Leads pour in, and investigations have to be conducted on the chance that the case involves more than just a lost person. After about the third day, we begin to get calls from people who have received thoughts or visions as to the victim's whereabouts, and we try to check these out as best we can. Sometimes, though not usually, these people are fairly close. I should mention also that many businesses make generous donations in the form of food or equipment during these large searches, and we certainly do appreciate their help.

Eventually, after all the leads have been followed through and everything humanly possible has been done in making the search itself, a search winds down. Yet an unsolved case always remains open, even though the search has been suspended.

I imagine that by now, most readers are convinced that we do not find anybody who is lost. Not true. I guess my point in describing several unresolved searches is that, like it or not, occasionally someone goes into the Maine woods and does not come out. Actually, our batting average is extremely high. Hunters make up the largest number of people who get lost. Others include hikers, berry-pickers, brook fishermen, etc., but the hunter, by sheer volume of participants, has the greatest chance of becoming lost.

A routine (if there is such a thing) "lost hunter" call might go like this: You have just gotten home for supper. The phone rings. It is a man from somewhere telling you he is at a pay phone. He and his buddy went hunting that morning. When he got back to the car at dark, no buddy. Yes, he fired his rifle and got no answer. You agree to meet him and try to find his chum. You hang up. *Damn!* There go the plans for tonight on that night-hunting tip you got today.

After meeting the caller at his camp, you get a description and other necessary information concerning his lost partner. Yes, he had matches, warm clothes, and a compass, and probably about fifteen cartridges for his rifle. Together with the rest of the party from camp, you go to the area where the man was last seen. This area turns out to be one where hunters frequently get lost, and usually come out that night or the next morning on the back road.

One of the party goes with you around to the back side, while the rest stay put. When you get there, you fire, and you get an answering shot. Good. A compass bearing and a twenty-minute hike brings you to the hunter. He has a fire going. In half an hour, you are back to the road. He knows where he went wrong in there, and you agree. The worst thing this guy can expect now is the fun his chums will poke at him back at camp.

Sometimes, unfortunately, the situation is very different. Occasionally, a completely well-adjusted person will suddenly realize for the first time in his life that he does not know where he is. Up until now he has known, for every moment of his existence, the precise location of everything he has needed, and his own orientation. This is just the kind of person who can really begin to panic when he realizes he is lost, and it is then that the trouble begins. When the panic button is pushed, the reason switch goes off. If the panic becomes really serious, sometimes a person actually begins to run, and, as he heats up, will shed the clothes that would save him.

It is not a pretty sight to see someone who has come unglued from panicking in the woods. Panic can lead to several things—injuries being one. The greatest danger, undoubtedly, is hypothermia. Panic probably would not kill you; hypothermia can, and, in fact, is usually what does lost people in. As the body cools down, the thought processes slow and allow hallucinations. We have found hunters wandering about in a daze many days after becoming lost. One man in particular, I remember, had crossed several roads in a week's time, and did not recall any of them. Supervisor Dave Priest recalls one lost hunter in a pretty peculiar state. He had been out several days when Dave found him. When Dave asked him where his gun was, he stated that "the little green men from Baxter Island" had come and taken his gun and knife away. You know a person in this condition is not going to make it much longer on his own.

We stress to people in our training courses the importance of remaining calm and building a fire should they become lost. If they will build a fire and stay put, we will find them fairly quickly. There is no way to know how many lost people's lives have been saved by wardens over the years. I can assure you, there are a great many.

For our first hundred years, the methods used by wardens to find lost persons remained basically unchanged. In 1982, a significant new approach was added. I would like to relate how this came about, and what it has meant to us.

As the trend toward outdoor activities in Maine took off over the past several years, we found ourselves involved in a tremendously increased number of searches. We found ourselves looking for cross-country skiers, snowmobilers, hikers, nature-lovers, bird-watchers—anyone who turned up missing or overdue. Depending on the nature of the incident, it became rather unclear at times just which agency should be the primary agency to respond. Unfortunately, sometimes, conflicts arose that lent a somewhat unprofessional aspect to a matter. Eventually, wisdom prevailed, and in 1982 a law was passed that designated the Warden Service as the primary agency to handle all searches and rescues in the fields and forests of Maine. Many meetings and hours later, letters of mutual agreement were worked out between agencies, sheriff's departments, state police, search-and-rescue teams, etc., as to what the role of each would be in various situations. It certainly has worked well, I feel. Each agency is familiar with the various resources available in other agencies, as well as whom to contact to obtain these in matters of urgency. Sometimes one agency will have a supportive role in assisting another in an incident, such as a plane crash. This agreement was a great step in the right direction.

The Maine Warden Service made a large step of its own at about the same time. Since so much time is expended each year on searches, it was felt that if any training were available along these lines, we should have it to keep up with our newly acquired role.

In September 1982, thirty warden lieutenants and sergeants got some expert schooling. The National Park Service, in conjunction with the National Association for Search and Rescue (NASAR), held a weeklong training session at the Maine Criminal Justice Academy in Waterville. As a result of this training, we now utilize the very latest techniques on a search that goes into an extended status. It would not be practical to explain the whole system. But I think the basic concept and how it was arrived at is fascinating.

During the early 1970s, a Mr. William S. Syrotuck, an experienced search manager, began to gather information from around the country regarding lost persons. Each state that could do so

provided him with case reports on various searches and their out-
comes. He felt strongly that people are all the same, and that if one
could categorize them, certain behavioral patterns would show up.
Taking his information, he began to break it down and feed it into
a computer.

The results showed that he was right. People from all over,
depending on what category they fell into, generally exhibited
somewhat similar behavioral patterns in regard to what they did
upon becoming lost and how far away they were, when found,
from the place they were last seen. Putting these people in various
categories of age and ability (such as children one to six years old,
children six to twelve years, elderly people, hunters, hikers, retarded people, etc.) and crossing this data with the type of terrain they
were in (hilly, flat, mountainous, etc.) made it possible to predict
with an amazing degree of accuracy the distance they could be
found from where they were last seen.

In conjunction with this information, charts and formulas
were worked out indicating how best to utilize the available
resources to find a given person. Once a profile has been made on
a particular lost person, he will fall into one of the standard categories, and the nature of the search for him will be based on this.

If you can imagine trying to manage several hundred people
on a major search, several miles back in the woods, using the hood
of your truck for your field desk and the cab for a command post,
you can visualize the inadequacies involved. For starters, you have
everyone's spilled coffee and fly dope all over your maps, reporters
pestering you for info, and a dozen other things all detracting from
your effort.

As a result of this schooling in a more scientific approach, we
were able to resolve most of these problems. First, the state was

separated into two zones, North and South. Two teams were chosen to respond to and manage any major search. Each team has a leader or search boss, along with a warden to handle each of the other roles: communications officer, plans officer, support services officer, and operations officer. Each warden has a specific job at the scene.

We now have a mobile command post that is brought to the scene of a major search or drowning. Complete with heater, electric generator, and refrigerator, it is a far cry from the hood of a vehicle. A converted camper/trailer, it serves us very well as a field office, where maps can be studied and plans formulated without interference.

The way people manage to get lost does not seem to have changed much at all, but we have changed the way we go about finding them. I think that the Maine Warden Service takes a backseat to no one when it comes to knowing how to quickly and effectively mount a search effort for those who become lost. We sure have had a lot of practice.

SEARCH FOR LOST PERSONS IN MAINE FOR 20-YEAR PERIOD

July 1–June 30	Persons Lost
1959–60	323
1960–61	206
1961–62	231
1962–63	429
1963–64	577
1964–65	494
1965–66	662
1966–67	452
1967–68	455
1968–69	473
1969–70	444
1970–71	361
1971–72	391
1972–73	349
1973–74	390
1974–75	457
1975–76	346
1976–77	265
1977–78	270
1978–79	302
1979–80	302
1980–81	308
Average	**385**

6 — KATAHDIN

You may well wonder what place Mount Katahdin has in a book about Maine game wardens. Well, it is a good question—and I have some good answers.

According to several sources, on a clear day there is more land mass visible from Katahdin than from any other mountain in the United States. Although only a mile high, it sticks out like the proverbial sore thumb, and can be seen for miles and miles. It breaks an otherwise more or less flat terrain that covers all of central and northern Maine.

Katahdin's uniqueness has been discussed and written about many times by many people, with good reason. It is undoubtedly the most striking piece of real estate in all of Maine—but it will never again be for sale, since Percival P. Baxter's purchase and gift of Katahdin and the surrounding wilderness territory included provision that it remain "forever wild" for the people of Maine. The most awesome feature of Mount Katahdin, in my opinion, is the weather. New Hampshire's Mount Washington reportedly attracts the worst weather known on Earth. Because of similar characteristics, including latitude, comparisons between Mount Washington and Mount Katahdin indicate that both peaks share pretty much the same weather conditions.

The Indians held Katahdin in awe and fear. It was their belief that the evil god Pamola dwelt on the mountain, and they feared his wrath should they venture into his domain. Many superstitions had their beginnings in some incident that through years of telling became distorted, and I can easily believe that a group of Indians may have ventured onto the mountain one nice fall day years ago in quest of the caribou that were moving up to their winter range on the Tableland. Without warning, a tremendous storm must have engulfed them and they perished, leaving others to speculate, and thus adding fuel to their belief in Pamola. In modern times, unfortunately, Pamola has swung his mighty club several times—and believe me, he can hammer you without much in the way of warning.

October 28, 1963, was a most typical Indian summer day on Mount Katahdin. Although Baxter State Park was officially closed, Mrs. Helen Mower and Mrs. Margaret Ivusic, both from Massachusetts, had received permission to hike to the summit. They left Chimney Pond around seven a.m., and spent the day enjoying the scenery and basking in the warm sun as they made their way up Cathedral Trail to the summit. After having lunch on Baxter Peak, they began to cross the Knife Edge to Pamola Peak. Margaret Ivusic was some distance ahead when Helen Mower heard her call from below her, "Come this way—it's a shortcut." It did not appear to be a shortcut to Helen Mower. She was apprehensive about leaving the trail, so continued to Pamola and down Dudley Trail to Chimney Pond.

When she arrived back at the campsite at around 6:30 p.m., no one was there. She built a fire and waited. Around 8:15 p.m., Ranger Ralph Heath returned to his camp at Chimney Pond, and Helen related the story to him. Heath went to a place where he could, by hollering, communicate in the still night air with Mrs.

Ivusic. She told him she was on a wall and could not go up or down. Heath left Chimney Pond again at around eleven p.m. to try to reach the stranded woman. Around four a.m. he returned, saying he had again been unable to reach Mrs. Ivusic.

Heath rested and had breakfast. The wind had begun to blow and snow to fall. Ralph radioed Supervisor Helon Taylor around six a.m., stating that if the woman was going to be saved, it would have to be now. Again he left, with his gear and warm clothing for Mrs. Ivusic. Mrs. Mower watched him disappear into clouds of swirling wind and snow for the last time. Ralph Heath gave his life in the finest tradition, attempting to save another.

By the time rescuers were able to reach Chimney Pond, a full-fledged arctic blizzard was raging and wiped out any trace of the two. Warden Elmer Knowlton and Ranger Rodney Sargent made a tremendous effort to reach the spot, but were turned back by the weather. Elmer suffered a badly wrenched knee from which he never completely recovered. Then began the long winter's wait until spring, when the snows would melt and the full story could be pieced together.

During that winter, wardens Donald Gray and Roger Spaulding were sent to New York State to receive some training in ice climbing, in anticipation of the chore that lay ahead come spring. Later that winter, they were on the mountain instructing other wardens in the techniques they had learned. The nucleus of our eventual rescue team had taken shape.

In late April, the snows began to melt, and it was time. Wardens Elmer Knowlton and Charlie Merrill made the long trek onto Pamola and began to scan below for any sign of the missing ranger and woman. Finally, with binoculars, Elmer spotted a rope hanging over an outcropping of rock far below.

The team of wardens was contacted. Then began the arduous

task of locating the bodies, freeing them from their icy tombs, and transporting them off the mountain. Margaret Ivusic's body was located near the rope. It was apparent that Heath had in fact reached her, and had placed her with warm clothing in a more sheltered spot. It took several days to remove the woman's body from the ice, each day making the strenuous trip up and down the mountain. Finally, she was freed. Then came the backbreaking task of transporting the body back up to the Knife Edge, across to Baxter Peak, then down to Thoreau Spring. It was here that a large helicopter was able to pick up the body and remove it from the mountain.

Ralph Heath's body was not found until some time later, when the ice and snow had receded further. The procedure was repeated once more. This whole evacuation took place during the most hazardous time of all—during the spring, when ice and snow are melting, and there is ever-present danger of ice and rock fall. The higher the angle involved, the greater the danger to those below. These rock and ice falls, along with snow slides, have been the death of many a climber throughout the world.

What would have to be called a bruising, exhausting job was pulled off in terrific fashion by game wardens and park rangers. But this incident appeared to trigger a series of incidents around and on the mountain. The following year, two men slept one night in their vehicle at Roaring Brook. Before daylight, one of them left on foot, telling his companion he was climbing the mountain to watch the sun rise. The next time anyone saw him, his bones were discovered behind a log on the back side of Basin Pond. The year after that saw us involved in the search for the Mott brothers. Was there no end to Pamola's wrath?

One evening in July 1966, I received a call from my supervisor,

Dave Priest, reporting an injured climber on Katahdin. I gathered my gear and left Grindstone to meet team member Glenn Speed from Haynesville. We met and struck off for Katahdin. Forty-five minutes later we were at Roaring Brook, then headed for Chimney Pond. I always dreaded that 3.3-mile hike to Chimney Pond, but it went quickly this night, and we arrived about 9:30 p.m. There was a strange tenseness about the place, as there usually is when you have what is known as "a situation."

Sixteen-year-old Jim Ludwig told us of the day's climb he and his father, Charlie, had made. Partway across the Knife Edge, his father had wanted to take what had appeared to be a shortcut to Chimney Pond. They had descended quite some distance, when, while trying to descend a waterfall, his father had slipped and fallen. Jim had been able to reach his father and determine that he was badly injured and unable to move. He then returned to the Knife Edge and down to report the incident. The boy was very calm, but due to his unfamiliarity with the mountain, could not pinpoint the exact location for us.

At that point, we received word via radio that the rest of our team would arrive early in the morning. Shortly afterward, Glenn and I left for Pamola Peak. As we climbed in the dark, I began to understand why the Indians dreaded this place; I was beginning to dread it, too. We arrived on Pamola at 12:45 a.m. Winds were fairly still, but we got into our sleeping bags behind a rock windbreak to await daylight. As dawn came, the air became very still. The whole world as far as you could see looked as though someone had packed it in cotton batting and left just the tops of a few hills poking up through. It was a tremendous sight.

Very soon we began to work our way across the Knife Edge, hollering for Charlie as we went. Almost immediately, we could hear his voice from far below trailing upward in the still air. The problem was, it sounded like it was coming from several different places. The echoes would not let us pinpoint his location. We continued across until we both agreed that he was directly below us somewhere, then started down. At five a.m., guided by his yells, we had reached a point where we could see him. He had slipped and fallen about twenty-five feet straight down, and was lying on his back in a shallow pool of water. At his back was the cliff he had fallen from; a short distance in front of him was another vertical drop of an unknown distance.

We immediately rigged up and rappelled down to the injured man. I have observed people who were glad to see someone, but I believe he had to take first place. We were greatly relieved to learn that he was all right. Aside from being extremely cold, he was in good spirits. It appeared that he had suffered a broken leg and shoulder in the fall; fortunately, the cold water had kept the pain to a minimum. It did not take long to assess the situation and know that it was going to take a lot of help to extricate Charlie Ludwig from his predicament, 1,500 feet below the Knife Edge.

Glenn decided that the quickest way to get back to Chimney and report the seriousness of the situation would be to continue down from this point. We would need more help than we knew was coming up the mountain. After placing an anchor pin, he took my rope along with his and dropped off in front of me on a long rappel. Eventually, he called for the rope. I unclipped it, and it, too, disappeared from view.

I quickly went to work, trying to make Charlie more comfortable. There was nowhere to put him other than where he was, in the water; the sides were too sloping. After splinting his leg and trying to make his shoulder more comfortable, there was not much to do but wait. (I did have some pain tablets, which he took; but after the ordeal was over, he wrote me and acknowledged that it was my "vocal anesthesia" that did the most good.)

Anyway, we began to get acquainted as the hours passed. Several times, I helped him change his position in an attempt to make him more comfortable. We wrapped his leg in my raincoat and propped it up under my rolled-up sleeping bag to keep it out of the water. The hours dragged by. By ten o'clock, I began to listen and watch anxiously for the rescue team. Our conversation ran primarily as to how we would get him out of the chasm. I kept telling him we would get him out that day, but I was beginning to be not so sure. Concerns about the possibility of Glenn's having fallen began to tug on my mind.

Around noon, clouds began to roll in and the wind began to blow and the sky grew black. My hopes of pulling off the evacuation that day vanished. Suddenly, it was raining harder than I ever thought possible. Lightning and thunder seemed to come all at once and were striking every several seconds. It was ear-shattering at times. In less than five minutes, the previously innocent little trickle of water at our backs had become a roaring waterfall. It was cascading onto Charlie, and there was no place to relocate him. Small rocks were bouncing around everywhere as if flung by an unseen hand. I heard several strike my hard hat, which I had placed on Charlie's head. I watched the brink of the falls, expecting a large rock at any moment, but it never came. The storm, instead of passing, only grew worse. It was extremely cold, and by now Charlie's shivering resembled convulsions.

The wind was curling the water from the falls in front of us back into our faces. The noise from the wind, lightning, and thunder was unbelievable. The mountain seemed to literally tremble with each lightning strike. Charlie was praying out loud and asked me to do the same. By now, I knew we were in grave danger. I recognized the signs of advancing hypothermia in myself. The most startling thing I recall in that regard is that, as I watched for the rescuers, I several times saw bushes move and thought they were people. It was then that I knew I must leave if I could. Charlie had pleaded with me several times to leave and save myself. I had studied the left-hand wall for a long time even before the storm struck, and knew it could be used to escape if one had to. That was before standing on a rock for eight hours and shivering.

Suddenly Charlie hollered. The water had risen enough, and the flow had started him toward the brink in front of us. Quickly I braced him with my knee. That damned storm had apparently found a home and was not about to leave. Several times Charlie begged me to go. At one point, he asked the Lord to take him. It was a tremendously hard thing to see a man go through. If I left, or tried to, I knew the water would move him.

Finally, at three o'clock, I knew I had to leave, or possibly two people would die instead of one. The rock on which I had been standing was not large, so I was able to roll it through the water to where Charlie was. By maneuvering around, he was able to brace his good leg against it and hold his position. I told him I was leaving and would be back, if possible, with help. I told him to hang on with all he had. As I turned to leave, he thanked me, and said, "If I don't make it, Eric, tell my wife and son I prayed for them."

Moving up and out around the edge of the crevice we were in, I looked back just before the next move would take me out of sight. He waved back; then I rounded the corner. In my heart, I guess I felt we would not see him again, alive. He had been through so much, and he knew he could end it by simply relaxing.

By good fortune, I was able to get back around, and began working back up toward the Knife Edge. Although it seemed impossible, the weather began to worsen even more. Once I had left the protection of the gorge, the wind was brutal. It had gotten colder and was now sleeting. The sleet was being driven at a great velocity, and it felt like the flesh was being sandblasted from my face. By sheltering my eyes with one hand, however, I could make way. It was really crazy. Lightning was striking every few seconds somewhere, and quite often too close for comfort. I can remember looking ahead at rocks and wondering whether I would get to them or be struck. The lightning danced about everywhere.

After a while, I approached the Knife Edge, and wondered what I would do when I got there. Traveling across it would be impossible. Suddenly, I saw something move. For some damned reason that I cannot explain, it appeared to be a monkey in a yellow rain suit. Donald Gray's wife has gotten a big laugh over the years about this. Anyway, that is who it was, along with the rest of the rescue team. There were also several wardens. Everyone had been pinned down, unable to move for several hours. Glenn had returned with them to show them where we'd descended.

The storm continued with fury for some time longer, and we waited in the relative calm just over the lip of the Knife Edge. Lightning continued its random walking about, blasting funny, jagged places in the rock here and there. Occasionally, a fat little blue spark would work its way up a portable radio antenna. One fiberglass rock helmet simply cracked. It was not a good place to be.

Eventually, the sleet and lightning abated, leaving only the wind. When I say wind, I am talking about the kind where you have to hang on to someone to keep from being blown over and landing in the rocks. Team members Don Walker and Don Gray and several volunteers made their way down over the side around five p.m. Charlie was still there. They lowered down to him, then put dry clothes on him and got him into a Stokes litter. Using a piton, they raised the litter up out of the water. They gave him some food, and secured a poncho over him. There were not enough people, equipment, or remaining daylight to effect a rescue before dark. Glenn and I left for Chimney Pond.

The following morning we were back on the mountain in force with ropes and volunteer rescuers, including wardens and park rangers. The wind was fairly gusty, but at least the sun shone. We were packaging Charlie for his evacuation by eight o'clock. The first hurdle, the 25-foot vertical pitch behind him, went fairly smoothly. Then came the backbreaking 1,500-foot lift to the Knife Edge. We had given him some strong pain-killing medicine before we began, and had to give him some more on several rest stops. A 180-pound man is not the easiest thing in the world to carry, especially in conditions such as those. Despite attempts not to, we jostled him several times; it was obvious that it hurt, but he remained silent each time.

Taking turns being clipped into the litter, we were a little over four hours getting back to the Knife Edge with our cargo. It was then by no means over. In another four hours, we were across the Knife Edge to Baxter Peak. From there it was a relatively easy carry to Thoreau Spring, where a large military helicopter airlifted him to the Millinocket Hospital. Even though the walk to Chimney Pond and down to Roaring Brook was a long one, it was made easier knowing that despite everything Pamola could muster, we had pulled it off safely.

In addition to his injuries, Charlie Ludwig suffered a mild

case of pneumonia from his ordeal. He made a full recovery, and returned later to climb Katahdin again. This time, there were no shortcuts.

Wardens have gone to Katahdin several times to assist park rangers. Once in the night we helped carry down a boy who had been killed in a fall near Cathedral Trail. On another occasion, we went with rangers to help bring down a boy who was dazed by lightning on the Knife Edge. A storm had struck, and lightning had knocked down several people in two different parties. Most were only stunned, but the boy was knocked unconscious and was not breathing. His father had revived him with mouth-to-mouth resuscitation, but he'd been blinded. His vision eventually returned. Several people spent the night in tents on the mountain and were escorted down the following day.

I do not suppose there remains any doubt in anyone's mind at this point as to what Katahdin is capable of dealing out to those who tempt the gods. This following episode is offered not so much because wardens were involved as it is to illustrate the unbelievable courage and will to live that men are capable of exhibiting in the face of death. Mountain climbers around the world are unique in many respects. They accept the risks of their sport. Death is a constant companion to mountain climbers. The risks taken are worth the exhilaration and sense of accomplishment felt when a summit is gained. Most of the time you win; sometimes you lose. They accept this fact unquestionably, and most do not feel at all compelled to explain to a non-climber why they do what they do.

Late in the evening of January 31, 1974, Warden Carter Smith, myself, and our wives drove northward on Interstate 95 from Augusta, where we had been to a retirement party. It had gotten terribly cold, and the wind was blowing wildly. Several times, Christmas-tree-sized tops of large firs blew across the road in front of us, some seeming never to touch the ground. We remarked several times that it would be a damned poor night for a man to be caught out. Little did we know that, in fact, six climbers were caught out in the worst place of all—Mount Katahdin.

The following morning dawned crystal clear, with below-zero temperatures and a tremendous, never-ceasing wind. At one p.m., rescue team member Daniel Watson called and advised that Baxter Park supervisor Buzz Caverly had called for help. Something had gone afoul, and a six-man climbing group was in serious trouble on the mountain.

As quickly as possible, Supervisor Leonard Ritchie, Specialist Watson, Warden Davis, and myself headed for the Millinocket Airport to meet Buzz and a 112th Medevac helicopter from Bangor. When we arrived, details of the incident were still vague. We went quickly to Park Headquarters to await further radioed information from the Chimney Pond ranger. Shortly, we learned that one of the climbers had reached Roaring Brook Campsite; two rangers would transport him to Avalanche Field if the helicopter could pick him up. The helicopter left immediately, and we went to the hospital to help upon their return. Within a few minutes, it returned, and we carried the severely hypothermic victim to the emergency room. He appeared to be in very rough shape and did not speak. We were still uncertain as to where other members of the party were, or their condition. Before long, more news arrived. The leader of the group, Robert Proudman, had reached Chimney Pond. Two more also had been picked up, and all were being transported to the hospital, all in very serious condition from frostbite.

At this point, all we knew for sure about the situation was

that there were still two climbers on the mountain in serious condition. It was quickly decided that Dan Watson and myself would be flown to Chimney Pond to assist, if possible, in locating the missing two. We loaded our gear and took off.

Upon nearing the mountain, the strong winds became even more powerful. The pilot made several attempts, and each time we were turned away short of Chimney Pond. "It's no use," he stated. "Too dangerous." We agreed wholeheartedly, and told him if he could land again at Avalanche Field, we would walk. He tried his damnedest to land the plane, and it was impossible—the wind was just too strong. Finally, he got down to about four feet. The crew chief opened the door, and with an "out" jerk of his thumb, we were suddenly on foot in the blowing snow. By the time we dragged our gear clear, he was gone from hearing.

The pilot told me later that this trip was the worst he had ever had, including Vietnam. "I did everything I know how to do to land a helicopter, and it just wouldn't land. I was registering fifty knots while we were hovering." I am glad I did not know about all that until later.

It was now 4:30 p.m. as we began the long walk up to Chimney Pond. The wind was unbelievable. It shrieked and moaned in the hardwood trees like a never-ending procession of overhead jet planes. Normally, when you climb, you can shed some clothing; not this time. Crossing Basin Pond was nearly impossible. We had to hang onto each other and walk backwards. Dan had stopped several times, complaining of severe cold and discomfort around a certain area of his anatomy. I finally got my light and checked him out. By hollering in his ear, I suggested that perhaps if he zipped up his fly, it might help. He did, and it did.

We reached Chimney Pond at seven p.m. Several seconds

before we arrived, rangers had answered a thumping at the door. They had assumed it was us, since they knew we were on our way up. When they opened the door, however, a badly frozen climber toppled in. Dan and I arrived moments later. Paul DiBello's face, hands, and feet were quickly tended to. His eyes were frostbitten and quickly became very painful as the warmth returned. After bandaging his eyes, we began to remove his boots. His feet were frozen rock-solid to the top of his boots. Due to the seriousness of his condition, we decided that despite outside conditions, we would evacuate him immediately. Park Headquarters was notified by radio, and we asked that a rescue sled and personnel meet us at Roaring Brook to continue taking the victim to Togue Pond, where an ambulance could transport.

Paul was coherent and, as we prepared him for the evacuation, answered questions for us. The six climbers had spent the night trapped by a sudden temperature drop and howling winds on a small shelf. In the morning, he and another climber, Tom Keddy, were unable to attempt to continue upwards on the remaining pitch toward Pamola Peak. The other four had left to get help for him and Tom. By three p.m., no help had returned, and Paul felt that he was surely freezing to death. At this point, Tom was incoherent and unable to stand. Paul had tried to haul Tom up, but just could not do it. In what had to be the greatest display of sheer guts and the will to live, Paul had gotten himself to the ridge and stumbled down the mountain in the dark with frozen eyes and on two frozen feet. Later, it was found that he had fallen considerable distances on several occasions in his effort. Either by instinct or miracle, he reached Chimney Pond. He went to several lean-tos, unable to tell which building was which. By luck, he eventually saw the light in the ranger's camp, and stumbled to it.

After packaging Paul in warm down sleeping bags and parka, we quickly began the trip down. Frequently we stopped to check his condition, then continued on. The sliding rescue litter worked fine, and we made the descent with no trouble. Before reaching Roaring Brook, we met the party that had started up to meet us. They took the litter and headed back down to the waiting rescue sled.

It was not yet over. Rangers Arthur York, Barry McArthur, Charles Kenney, Lon Pingree, Dan, and I began the long hike back to Chimney Pond. I thought I had a pretty good idea of what tired was, but I really did not. Heavy clothing and cold air greatly reduce one's efficiency. We arrived back at 11:30 p.m. and learned that Paul had arrived at the Millinocket Hospital. We also learned that the remainder of our Warden Service team would arrive at daylight, and that two more teams were on their way up to Chimney Pond that night.

Within a short time, the Eastern Mountain Sports rescue team from North Conway, New Hampshire, and a team from Augusta headed by George Smith arrived. It was now after midnight. There was some discussion of making an attempt to reach Keddy that night; however, after evaluating all the information we had, we decided that the risks to the rescuers were too high. The temperature was minus-20 degrees. A handheld wind-velocity device showed wind speeds of 40 to 50 mph. Just before daylight, the wind let up for a while, and soon the familiar *whop-whop–whop* and roar of the big Huey was heard over the camp. It made a quick landing on the pond with part of the Warden Service team. In a second, it was gone, returning shortly with the remaining members.

The teams quickly made ready for the attempt to reach Keddy. The wind quickly regained its velocity as the sun came up.

Unfortunately, neither Dan nor I was able to be of much assistance following our eleven-mile hike up and down the mountain. We wished them well and watched them go, carrying a litter and all their gear.

At approximately ten a.m. we received word that the Eastern Mountain Sports team had reached Keddy's position and that he was dead. Due to the high winds and cold, it was impossible to make the recovery that day. The body was secured, and the teams began the descent.

Team member Charlie Merrill recalls how treacherous the conditions were. The litter was often held in a horizontal position by the wind while someone was holding on to one end. The possibility of being blown off your feet and rolled by the wind was very real. The thought of losing a mitten in such conditions was nightmarish. Luckily, all returned without injury.

Several days later, when the weather broke, Tom Keddy's body was brought up to the ridge below Pamola Peak and evacuated by helicopter.

The circumstances leading to the ill-fated climb were soon related by the five survivors. Again, the villain was the weather that sometimes changes so suddenly on mountains. All six climbers were members of the Appalachian Mountain Club and had excellent qualifications and the expertise to be involved in winter climbing. Katahdin offers probably the best winter climbing, especially ice, in the eastern United States. It is these conditions that draw climbers from all over to Katahdin in winter.

Like many mountain climbers before him, Tom Keddy lost his life doing what he loved. He knew and accepted the risks. Climbers Page Densmore, Robert Proudman, Doug George, and Mike Cohen recovered from their ordeal. Paul DiBello lost both feet due to frostbite. He continues his life with style, in the manner you might expect from someone who displayed so much courage and the will to live against such horrendous conditions.

In recent years, it has become rare for Pamola *not* to make his presence known. On one occasion, a camper was killed by lightning in his tent at Chimney Pond. An ice climber was strangled by his own equipment in a fall while climbing the treacherous icy Chimney itself. In 1984, two climbers perished when engulfed in an avalanche.

Game wardens joined the Baxter State Park rangers several times on Mount Katahdin in the past. The rangers now handle these occurrences, usually unassisted, and have established an excellent record in doing so. To say the least, Mount Katahdin is one hell of a pile of rocks, and—to quote former rescue team member Charlie Merrill—"One hell of a place to find out if your ice ax really will stop you when you begin to slide."

7 — RESCUE

From time to time you glance upwards, hoping to see some blue sky. "Damn!" you say to yourself. "This is going to be a long one, I'm afraid." Your younger wardens have gone on ahead, and you hate to admit it to yourself, but you are not as young as you used to be. After a short breather, you push on up the trail. You estimate you have covered about three miles—good, only two to go. You keep thinking about that chopper on the ground at Carrabassett, hoping somehow there will be a break in the fog so that it can come.

Finally, you reach the Appalachian Mountain Club shelter on Spaulding Mountain, and a very concerned group of young hikers is gathered about the lean-to. The teenage girl inside fell and hurt her leg, and is unable to walk. Here on the mountain it is very foggy and damp, but you are advised by portable radio that the weather is clear on the other side, and they are just waiting. Together with the men you set a deadline. After a certain time, you will start the long carry down on foot. Your back begins to ache already. It is then you begin to take a closer look at her friends and pick out the beefy ones; there is no such thing as too many people when it comes time to carry someone on a litter off a mountain.

In a few minutes, someone hollers, "Hey, look!" Sure enough, a small patch of blue appears for a second or two. Within a short time, the conditions have improved significantly. The chopper pilot says he will come when you think he can. Without waiting for the clouds to close in again, you give him the word to come now, then instruct the group to make ready. "Yes, I think we should remove that fir tree, and probably that one, just to be safe. Let's get everything around here like packs, raincoats, etc., secured so they won't be blown up into the chopper's rotors. Put the fire out, and wet down the remains. The hundred-mile-per-hour wind from the rotor wash of a hovering Huey can create havoc on the ground beneath it."

Everything is done. Within minutes, the familiar, unmistakable sound of beating rotors is heard . . . what a beautiful sound. Moments later, the noise is ear-shattering as the Huey hovers directly overhead. Soft-wood treetops thrash violently, and several snap off, and sand and grit sting your face as the wire litter is lowered. Quickly it is unsnapped, and the chopper retrieves the cable. The pilot moves away from the area a short distance until you are ready.

On the count of three, the injured girl is gently lifted and placed into the litter alongside her. She has been placed in a down sleeping bag and strapped in the litter. There is apprehension in her eyes—understandably—and you explain to her that the jacket must be placed over her head to protect her eyes. She nods, and forces a smile. Once the jacket has been secured, she is carried outside. Within seconds, the Huey has again taken its position overhead, and down comes the hoist cable. It touches the ground, and a warden attaches it to the bridle harness on the litter. Slowly, it begins to rise.

At this point, the metal roof on the shelter begins to lift from the tremendous turbulence, and several people run to lie down on it to keep it in place. Just as the litter comes beneath the skids of the chopper, it begins to spin like a top. Quickly, the crew chief is standing outside on the skid, and, secured by a harness, he stops the spinning litter with his foot. Within seconds, the litter is aboard the chopper and gone.

There is a hearty round of applause; then it is very quiet again. You re-lash your own collapsible litter to your pack frame. After rounding up the rest of the gear, you all head down the mountain. The boys from the 112th Medevac have come through again.

If I were to read the previous story without knowing where it happened, I might guess that it happened somewhere out west in a national park. But, no. Many people do not realize it, but such rescues have become almost commonplace now in Maine. Most rescues take place in the mountainous areas of western Maine, but this by no means includes all of them. Non-mountain rescue situations involving sick or injured people in remote areas have become fairly common, and wardens have often worked with various military units in incidents requiring emergency airlift.

Rescuing people might seem to be somewhat removed from the general duties of a game warden. I guess I would be inclined to agree with that, but we somehow grew into the role. In the past twenty-five years, as Maine's population has grown, more and more people have become involved in outdoor activities other than hunting and fishing—hiking, climbing, canoeing, whitewater rafting—and they seem to keep finding ways to get into scrapes.

In January of 1965, six wardens were selected to make up a new team specializing in rescue work. This occurred shortly after the incident on Mount Katahdin in which Margaret Ivusic and

Ranger Ralph Heath lost their lives, and the need for a trained mountain-rescue team was apparent. Another reason for forming the team was the increasing number of drownings each year. With so many Maine lakes and streams, the number of incidents was understandably high. Wardens spent many hours on recovery operations, and it was felt that divers would be more effective in these operations.

That winter found six of us attending the Bangor YMCA, taking scuba diving training. When time permitted, we also learned the aspects of technical mountain climbing and high-angle evacuations.

Sooner than we expected, it was obvious that more than six men were needed to handle the diving demands. More divers were trained, and joined the team; to their credit, they have recovered a remarkable number of drowned victims over the years. After twenty years, two of the original six wardens, Sergeant Don Gray and Specialist Charles Davis, are still diving. And, believe me, they can fill you in on some things that happen underwater.

Maine's lakes and ponds are not noted for their clarity. Forty feet down it is usually damned bleak. Divers are towed slowly behind a boat, utilizing a planing board, which operates much like the fins on a submarine. The diver hangs on, and by changing the angle is able to move up or down along the contour of the lake bottom. Too many times, there are snags or debris that, due to poor visibility, cannot be seen in time to be avoided.

Occasionally, the circumstances require diving under the ice. This is only slightly worse than you can possibly imagine. Going down through a hole in the ice into inky blackness with a rope around your waist is not something you look forward to. Regulators are prone to freeze up and not work properly—or, worse yet—even at all, in extreme conditions. If the area to be searched happens to be in a current, as it sometimes is—well, you can begin to get the picture. Luckily, no one has received serious injury.

Soon after it was formed, our mountain rescue team was involved in several rescues of a technical nature. (In mountain climbing jargon, technical involves the use of various aids, such as pitons and ropes, to assist and provide safety to the climber.) In addition to the Ludwig rescue on Katahdin, the team was twice called to evacuate stranded climbers on the face of Mount Kineo at Moosehead Lake. Frequently, inexperienced climbers will reach a point where it is impossible to continue up, then realize that they cannot climb down, either. The nearly vertical face of Kineo is a poor place to discover this fact.

After several years had passed, however, we had not been called on many subsequent rescues that actually required any great amount of technical expertise. We trained each year, but we knew we were not able to train to the extent we should. Baxter Park rangers had formed their own team and were capable of handling "situations" there. Several other teams had developed also, and had offered their help when the need should arise. The point was driven home by the Tom Keddy incident that there were other teams better trained and equipped than we were. These teams consisted of avid climbers, several of whom had climbed in other parts of the world. When you do this sort of thing, you should love it to the point that you are doing it in your free time.

None of us felt that compelled. Therefore, we decided that before someone got hurt, it would be best to phase out the mountain rescue aspect of the team.

In recent years, the Appalachian Trail has experienced a

tremendous increase in popularity, and the Border or Longfellow Mountains (depending on what name you choose) are now being hiked every month of the year. The extreme western part of the range, the Mahoosucs, seem to be the most popular of all. This is undoubtedly due to its rugged remoteness. The remoteness is fine; it is the ruggedness that creates the problems. Wardens in this area have become well acquainted with removing injured hikers from steep mountainsides, quite frequently in the dark. Without exaggeration, this can be best described as backbreaking, treacherous labor. I have seen more than one rescuer with a torn knee cartilage, caused by stumbling into a hole he could not see as he struggled on the back end of a litter.

I think the following story is uniquely interesting, but sad in a way. Responding to a call from the Appalachian Mountain Club headquarters in Pinkham Notch, New Hampshire, several wardens, plus myself, began the long climb onto Fulling Mill Mountain near the New Hampshire state line. Some hikers had found an injured woman and reported the incident that morning.

We soon met Edna Williams, age sixty-two, from Melrose, Florida. Edna was on a solo hike from Mount Katahdin to Georgia, she hoped.

Near the top of Fulling Mill, as dusk approached, she had slipped and fallen. With a broken leg, she managed to pitch her tent beside the trail and crawl into it. The following morning, some hikers discovered her plight.

As we carried her down, her grit and spunk became apparent as she told of her experiences along the trail. In many spots, the trail's steepness required a "hand down" to a group below; we apologized for the jostling, but she only grinned and said, "I know you're doing the best you can." In several hours, we reached the vehicles and placed her, litter and all, in the back of my truck. One hour later, after a slow trip over a rough road, we were on our way to the hospital in Rumford.

During her stay at the hospital, I called on her several times and did some errands for her, such as having money wired from home and buying magazines. One day, I asked her why, at her age, she had chosen such an endeavor. Sadly, she related her story. With an invalid daughter to care for, she had been pretty much house-bound for many years. The daughter had passed away, and she was now determined to do many things she had never been able to do. She had run a florist shop for years, and decided to take the Maine-to-Georgia trip so she could see and photograph the many different species of flora along the way.

When she was well enough to go home, to save her the long ambulance ride, my wife and I took her with her wheelchair to the Portland Jetport, and saw her off. "Don't worry," she said. "I'll be back. I'm going to start next year where I left off."

Early the next summer, she called one evening. "I'm at the home of the lady who was my nurse during my hospital stay," she said. "I'm leaving in the morning to continue on my journey." She was excited, and I wished her good luck.

The following day, Edna was on her way again until, on Fulling Mill Mountain again, she fell and broke the same leg in a different place. Again, wardens carried her down. This time, she spent several days hospitalized in Berlin, New Hampshire. Sadly, she admitted her hopes to walk the trail from Maine to Georgia would have to be abandoned. She sure gave it a good try.

If we are lucky and if weather permits, a helicopter can speed up the process of rescuing these people. In recent years, we have called on the 112th Medevac so frequently that often they know from past rescues where to go, and do not require a guide. Sometimes, when conditions will not permit using a hoist, we have had to transport the victim to a suitable landing spot. But those chaps sure can fly those machines. More than once on our rescues they have been unable to find a place big enough to land properly, so they half-landed with one skid resting on a large rock, the other on nothing. Understandably, they do not like to remain in these poses too long, so everything has to be ready to go when they arrive. There is a great deal of risk involved for the men who fly these missions; one sudden gust of wind at the wrong instant could spell disaster.

One fairly close call occurred in 1984 while we attempted to hoist a critically injured climber to a helicopter from Tumbledown Mountain (in Township 6, near Weld). The victim had fallen and received head injuries, from which he later died. It was impossible, due to the high angle and the seriousness of the injuries, to move the man to a better location. Some small trees in the immediate area were removed. As the litter was hoisted, it went into another small tree, but luckily did not snag.

I have lost track of exactly how many of these helicopter-assisted mountain rescues we have made in western Maine in recent years. At least eight come to mind, with three of those on Old Speck in Grafton Notch.

Since 1982, when the Warden Service became the primary agency in the search-and-rescue field, we have made some great strides in both respects. Through the efforts of Gary Anderson, Warden Service Search and Rescue Coordinator, many others outside of the Warden Service have become involved. Throughout the state there are now several search-and-rescue teams. We depend on them a great deal, and justly so. Most team members spend many hours in vigorous training each year, and have acquired an admirable degree of expertise. From time to time, we set up train-ing seminars for them. Making these as realistic as possible, we have included actual high-angle evacuations on Katahdin in winter, to test their technical skills on ice, as well as similar exercises in warmer weather. Military helicopters, Army, Navy, and Coast Guard, are always glad to participate. They, in turn, have set up training sessions to familiarize Search and Rescue (SAR) groups with the proper safety procedures regarding helicopters. These ses-sions have proven very worthwhile when an actual situation occurs. In an emergency, it is essential to know where the various rescue teams are, their areas of expertise, and their response times. It also saves precious time to have them know what we expect of them when they do arrive. These groups are our backbone, and we are damned glad to have them working with us.

The latest development in rescue work lies with the enor-mous increase in whitewater rafting. In just a few years since the first appearance of rafting in Maine, it has grown into a tremen-dously popular form of recreation. There are twenty-two licensed outfitters now conducting rafting trips down Maine rivers each year. Several wardens with these rivers within their districts have received training in rescuing rafters who may become stranded or injured. Despite its wild and exhilarating appearance, rafting is a fairly safe form of recreation. There are many strict regulations regarding safety equipment and procedures, and these help keep accidents to a minimum. The outfitters themselves are extremely safety-minded, and generally can take care of any situations that arise by themselves.

Wardens learn safe methods in the handling and use of dynamite and other explosives.

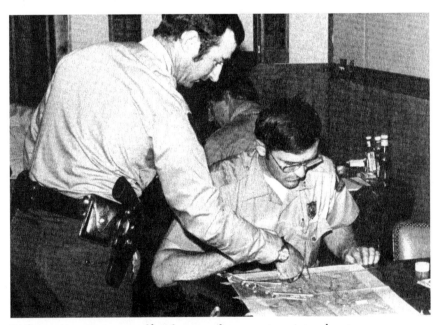

Proficiency in orienting oneself with map and compass is an integral part of warden training.

Wardens placing a suspected night hunter under arrest.

Wardens inspect an illegal trap set to catch deer.

Much of a warden's daily patrol takes place on the water.

Often the easiest—and sometimes the only—way to get into the back country is by float plane.

Rescues must be made in all conditions. Here, warden divers return from a search in freezing water.

Wardens searching for a drowning victim experience treacherous conditions at Steep Falls on the Saco River.

Ed Lowell entered the Warden Service in 1904. When he retired 46 years later at the age of 75, he was considered the dean of American game wardens.

Dealing with wildlife is all in a day's work for these two wardens.

Beaver dams can cause extensive flooding. Here, a warden breaks up a dam to release the flow of Sourdnehunk Stream.

Sometimes it's just more efficient to destroy a dam with explosives. Here, the author blows a dam with a charge of dynamite.

Coordinating a search.

Warden Pilot Jack McPhee locates his man.

Wardens rescue a pilot injured in a plane crash.

Prepping for a winter climbing rescue.

This rescue team is heading out for the Knife Edge on Katahdin.

These wardens have landed to check on a fishing party.

Chatting with an ice fisherman.

Wardens use canines to search vehicles for contraband, or signs of illegal game.

$\mathscr{8}$ — ALWAYS THE DANGER

More than once, I have left home in the morning wishing that something might happen to alter the routine a little. More than once, by the time I got home, I sorely regretted—and I do mean sorely—ever thinking along those lines.

Dark was approaching in the North Country. The temperature was well below zero, and a driving snowstorm was howling across Chesuncook Lake. A lone figure on snowshoes was trudging down the lake in near-zero visibility. Warden Dave Priest had his mind on the nice supper he would have when he reached home in a few minutes, when suddenly, he was floundering in thirty feet of water. Luckily, holding on with one hand, he was able to work both snowshoes off with the other. Each time, the ice broke as he tried to heave himself onto it. He finally made it onto the ice, stood up, took one step, and went in again. Finally, after repeating the process again, the ice held. Dave Priest cheated the Grim Reaper that night.

As with practically any other job, there are occupational hazards associated with being a game warden. The variety of these hazards is magnified by the fact that wardens, especially in the backcountry, are frequently alone, with no help for miles. Nearly every warden at some time or another has had an experience such as Dave's. Warden Norman Moulton once went through the ice on a snowmobile during the smelt run. Wardens Donis Wheaton and Charlie Davis broke through into the slush on Ross Lake one night while checking for set ice-fishing lines. Being stranded with wet feet at 24 degrees below zero is not exactly a picnic, to be sure. One might say, "Well, they shouldn't have been there in the first place." That is not the nature of a game warden's business, however.

In winter, wardens spend much time on the ice, checking fishermen and beaver traps. I know of few wardens who have not been through the ice around a beaver flowage. Fortunately, most of these are shallow. Airplanes are tremendous tools, and have been used in the Warden Service for years. Landing and taking off from small ponds or rough, snow-covered ponds occurs almost daily for some wardens. If you have ever experienced anything besides a normal landing in a lightplane, you know what this means. It is amazing how a pond seems to shrink when it is time to take off. Sometimes a warden will find himself in a snow squall, trying to get here or there, and have to work around it. There are few scenes bleaker than that seen from a lightplane window when snowflakes are zooming past; this is especially true in the mountains of western Maine, where I live. Some of the clouds around here have granite in them.

Dynamiting obstructing beaver dams—rescuing injured climbers—dealing with armed poachers, sometimes alone—it's all in a day's work for a game warden. Nothing is predictable. A game warden's business does become risky from time to time. We accept these risks, and try our best to minimize them in performing the various functions of the job, but we cannot eliminate them altogether.

Sometimes the risks are brought on by nature; at other times, by people. Nearly all wardens have had a gun pointed at them at some time or another. National statistics will bear this out. According to these statistics, a game warden is many times more likely to be assaulted during his career than any other type of law enforcement agent. The chances are also much higher that when it happens, it will be with a firearm. This is because a great percentage of people that wardens deal with are carrying firearms.

I mentioned earlier that most of the boundary wardens have had guns held on them. They by no means have the corner on the market. The following are but several firearm assaults of wardens in recent years. Although most of these incidents occurred in night-hunting situations, it is not always that way.

Warden Gary Pelletier was returning home from "working night hunters" several years ago. He had dropped off his partner, and was alone. Snow had begun to fall. Noticing fresh vehicle tracks at a late hour, he followed them up a side road until he came to a stopped vehicle. Thinking they might be having trouble, he approached the vehicle. Several men were in the process of peeling a safe stolen in a break. Before he realized this, however, a .357 magnum revolver was jammed into his stomach. The hammer snapped down on an empty chamber. In a reflex motion, he grabbed the weapon away and escaped into the woods. The subjects fled in the vehicle, firing several shots into the woods at Pelletier. One of the men suffered a critical gunshot wound as they made the escape in the car; indications were that it was accidentally inflicted by himself or one of the others. The perpetrators were apprehended later.

Warden Martin Savage had a similar escapade. A telephone

call at his home in Oquossuc reported that a vehicle had night-hunted a deer in the Wilsons Mills area and was headed for Oquossuc. Martin intercepted the vehicle, and had put the Canadian night hunters under arrest, when suddenly one of them held him at gunpoint. They walked him back to his car and disabled his radio. As they marched him back to their vehicle, he suspected he was going for a ride. In the dark, he managed to get a few steps ahead of them, then bolted for the ditch and escaped. His would-be captors fled, and were later apprehended by Canadian authorities.

Several years ago, Warden Jim Davis was patrolling a back road. He watched two subjects run from the vicinity of a camp to a vehicle and take off at a high rate of speed. As he pursued the vehicle, the passenger fired two shots through the rear window, both of which struck his hood. The subjects abandoned the car some distance away and, despite an all-night search by wardens, troopers, and sheriffs, they escaped. Some time later, both were eventually apprehended.

Many years ago, Warden Ed King was wounded in the arm by a poacher's bullet. He later lost the arm to frostbite, but continued to work with a hook. According to one retired warden, Ed once apprehended some fellows night-hunting outside a camp. After he arrested them, they all returned to the camp and went inside. It was here in the light that they noticed Ed's hook. One of the men said, "With only one arm, what would you do if we decided we weren't going with you?" King, who was standing near the door, turned and drove the hook into the door and ripped out a splinter about six inches long. "So far," he said, "no one has ever given me trouble."

Another close call happened in 1948. Warden Roland Abbot

of Bethel drove into a gravel-pit area to check out a vehicle. As he left his warden's vehicle, a man went quickly to the other vehicle and suddenly started firing with a .45 automatic. Before Abbot could reach the cover of his car, one round struck him on his backside. The man and the vehicle fled, and a search of all side roads and camps failed to turn up the car. Several days later, authorities in New York State had established a roadblock, suspecting that the armed man was headed that way. When he did show up, he attempted to run the block, and was killed by gunfire. Roland Abbot recovered from his wound. When authorities investigated what purpose the man had for being in the gravel pit, they discovered he was in the process of burying a dead cat. They also learned—not surprisingly—that the man had a history of mental problems.

Many times, the assault does not involve firearms, but is triggered when a person arrested suddenly decides it is "thump the warden" time. Phil Dumond has unpleasant memories of being whaled with an oar by some men standing in a boat. He was in the water, hanging onto the boat. "It was not too bad at first—they were hitting me with the flat part. I could take that pretty good. But Jesus Christ, pretty soon they started hitting with the edge. That hurt like hell, so I pulled out my little gun and hollered, 'Put down that goddamn oar, or I'll shoot you right between the eyes.' It worked. They put down the oar, and I did my business. Maybe I would have drowned if they had stunned me badly enough."

Wardens have also been run down by cars several times, as in the cases of Maynard Marsh, Irwin Bonney, and Wilbert Tupper. In recent years, several wardens have been injured by snowmobiles while attempting to stop them.

A prisoner suddenly turned violent as he was being hand-cuffed by Warden Ernest Smith. He lashed out and struck Smith's face with the free half of the cuff. It took some teeth and pierced his cheek from the inside—pretty harsh treatment.

I once thought I held the record for getting assaulted—being whaled on the head with a flashlight, kicked in the groin, kicked in the throat, bitten on the hand, punched in the eye, and attacked with a bumper jack. My inspector Bob Thomas and I were even assaulted once in a barn by an irate man on a tractor. That is a nightmarish story, and it can wait.

These things all go with the territory, you might say. Once, before I realized this, I was telling a good friend—Sergeant Harold Gallant, twenty-five-year veteran policeman on both the Millinocket and East Millinocket police forces—about the bumper jack incident. I am afraid I may have been looking for sympathy. But, when I was through, he only smiled and said, "You don't expect them to kiss you, do you?"

9 — THOSE WE LOST

Using dogs in deer hunting was an accepted method years ago. Due to the unsporting aspects, legislation was passed against this practice in the early 1880s, after which wardens frequently dealt with groups of men (nicknamed "daggers") who continued to hunt in this manner.

On November 8, 1886, Warden Lyman Hill and Deputy Charles Niles were in an area known as Fletcher Field, west of the Machias River. They confronted two men, Calvin Graves and a man named MacFarland, with strong evidence that Graves had been using his dog to hunt deer. A young boy who was present later testified to the following events: Warden Hill told Graves that he must seize the dog in question. He was told by Graves that if he did seize it, he would be shot. Niles leaned his rifle against the wagon on which Graves was seated and reached to untie the dog. As he did so, Graves loaded a shotgun and shot Deputy Niles in the head, killing him instantly. Graves then swung on Warden Hill, who had taken a few steps away, fired a second time, and struck Hill in the shoulder. Hill collapsed and died shortly thereafter.

At this point, the boy's father came from the woods. (The boy had run and hidden in an old well.) Graves told the father he had killed the wardens in self-defense, although the boy later testified that neither warden had raised a weapon. The murderer and his companion left, and the father, Tom McReavy, sent the boy to a nearby lumber camp while he went to Machias to report the incident. Warrants were issued for the two men immediately. MacFarland hid out in the woods for a period of time, but was frozen out and surrendered to authorities.

MacFarland was tried and acquitted. Graves fled, and was arrested the following March in San Francisco; the Bangor city marshal and a game warden went out west and brought Graves back to stand trial. He was convicted and sentenced to life imprisonment. Hill and Niles were the first Maine wardens to lose their lives in the line of duty.

In July of 1921, the son of Inland Fish and Game Commissioner Willis Parsons and Game Warden Arthur Deag were on a canoe trip on the West Branch of the Penobscot River. While attempting to run Pockwockamus Falls, they capsized. Young Parsons was able to get ashore, but Warden Deag was swept downriver and drowned.

Tragedy struck again rather quickly. On October 8, 1921, Warden Leslie Robinson was killed in a car wreck during a snowstorm. This occurred around the Ripogenus area in Township 2, Range 13. Another warden, Lloyd Hoxie, was injured in the wreck, but recovered.

One year later, in November 1922, came the disappearance and suspected murder of Supervisor David Brown and Warden Mertley Johnson, whose story was told in "The Boundary."

In May of 1933, Warden Baptiste Jalbert drowned on the St. Francis River. Jalbert and his cousin were proceeding upriver in a canoe. The water was high, and the spring drive was on, the river full of wood. The canoe struck a partially submerged log, upsetting the canoe. The cousin managed to struggle ashore, but Jalbert drowned.

In 1935, Warden Supervisor Robert Moore and Warden Lester Hale were proceeding south on an abandoned line of the Somerset Railroad Line, in an old car that had been converted to run on rails. When they reached Moscow, another vehicle struck them on a crossing. Moore was killed instantly; the other warden escaped injury.

In 1956, Warden Pilot George Townsend had just received a brand-new plane. Townsend, along with Nat Fellows, a department biologist, had just taken off from Maranacook Lake in Winthrop. The plane suddenly went into a stall and crashed, killing both men.

In 1968, Warden Lyle Frost was working on some nuisance beaver dams along a railroad bed. He had dynamited one dam, and was preparing to blow up the second, but a problem developed, and when Frost went to check the charge, it detonated, killing him.

Four years later, in 1972, and again at Maranacook Lake, tragedy struck. Warden Pilot Richard Varney had just taken off in a helicopter when the engine failed, and it dropped into the water. Dick managed to get out of the helicopter, but drowned before help arrived.

These were all good men who knew the risks involved and accepted the challenge.

10 — AIRCRAFT

Game wardens and aircraft go well together. With so many square miles of Maine lakes, streams, and forests to patrol, a warden in a plane can see in a few minutes more activities or evidence of activity than he could in many hours on the ground.

For many years, of course, wardens only dreamed of being able to see their districts from the air. It was, for the most part, the efforts of one man whose interest made the dream possible. During the late 1930s, Fish and Game Department Commissioner George Stobie became interested in flying. He also had acquired his own personal airplane, and frequently employed an ex–World War I pilot named Bill Turgeon as his pilot. Stobie was quick to realize the tremendous potential involved if wardens were able to fly. Bill Turgeon quickly became a valuable asset in Stobie's plans to put wardens in the air, and in 1939, Bill became the Warden Service's first pilot. Excellent qualifications, along with his tremendous enthusiasm for flying, made him an excellent choice. An Auburn native, Bill had attended MIT, as well as the US School of Military Aeronautics. He was still a very young man when World War I began. During the years 1918–19, he saw action as a member of the 13th Aero Squadron, Air Service, Aeronautics, and US Army.

Following the war, Bill got involved in commercial flying and several other aviation enterprises, including flight instruction. Aviation was growing rapidly everywhere during those years. In 1923, the Maine Aero Club was formed, and the membership voted him as its first president. His enthusiasm grew along with aviation's development, and seems to have touched off most of the early enthusiasm in Maine. In 1926, he became a member of the Aviation Regulation and Advisory Board. During the years 1928 to 1932, he served as the State of Maine's aeronautical inspector of aircraft. The following year, Governor Louis Brann appointed him to the post of state aviation advisor. If his enthusiasm for flying is not evident by now, consider this: During this time, he was also extremely busy for two years serving as superintendent in charge of the construction of the new Lewiston-Auburn Municipal Airport, as well as a member of the board of directors of Maine Aero Rendezvous Inc. Following the completion of the new airport, Bill became manager of Turgeon Airways. This enterprise found him flying everything from lightplanes to twenty-nine-passenger twin-engine airliners. Then, in 1939, thanks to George Stobie, Bill went to work for us, and wardens began to realize their dream.

A large five-place SR-10 Gullwing Stinson purchased by the commissioner was the first plane to fly game wardens to any extent. It was put on floats, however, which did not enhance its performance. Those who can remember it say it was built like a bridge, and flew like one. Nevertheless, wardens were quick to take advantage of this new tool, and Bill and the Stinson became a familiar part of their job.

By 1948, the Warden Service recognized the need to expand the services that planes could provide. Several wardens had become fliers under Bill's excellent tutelage, and were chosen to become flying wardens. Several of these first pilots were George Later, Wilfred Atkins, and Malcolm Maheu. Bill, naturally, was named chief pilot. The Gullwing Stinson had seen a lot of hours, and its lack of performance made it a less-than-ideal plane for the back-country when it came to getting in and out of the smaller ponds.

Smaller airplanes were becoming very popular at that time. They, too, were underpowered at best, but much more practical from a game warden's standpoint. These planes provided some unique experiences for our first pilots. George Later was at Ripogenus Dam when a newly acquired J-3 Cub was assigned to him. This airplane had only a 60-horsepower engine. George recalls jokingly, "You could take off in the morning into a stiff headwind, and at sunset still be where you started." Fuel was another problem—only twelve gallons of gas could be carried onboard. "We had five-gallon cans of gas stashed all over the North Country," says George. Wilfred "Sleepy" Atkins remembers the small amount of cargo one could carry. "Hell," he says, "you threw your hat in, and you were loaded."

Improvements seemed to come along much more slowly than the pilots had hoped. Horsepower slowly increased, but this was only one step in the right direction to the development of an ideal bush plane. Airplanes that live in warm hangars and take off and land on smooth runways have to be somewhat different, you might guess, from those that sit out all night at 30 degrees below zero and take off on bumpy, frozen lakes.

The term *Yankee ingenuity* is often heard, and it was this that the first warden pilots used in their efforts to develop a superior bush-type airplane. There was no denying Bill Turgeon's background and knowledge of flying. The most pressing problems were tackled first, and flying wardens, working under full approval of the Civil Aeronautics Administration, went to work. The Piper PA-12 was a tremendous little airplane; it was destined to become better. By installing a 125-horsepower engine, performance was greatly increased. One drawback to this plane's performance, however, was the lack of wing flaps—but this, too, was resolved. The pilots designed, then built their own; then, following the issuance of a supplemental-type certificate (similar to a patent), Marden Airways of Waterville installed them. The results were tremendous; pilots could now safely slow down to 45 mph, 15 mph slower than standard planes of the same model. This was a great advantage when using the low-and-slow approach to searching for lost hunters. It also added a definite safety improvement in a crisis situation by allowing a lower landing speed.

These early warden pilots, then, made numerous significant improvements—many of them in response to the challenges of Maine's weather, which can change drastically, pretty fast. Warm spells suddenly turn cold, causing condensation and freezing. In those days, planes came with a special wrench for unfastening the fuel-tank bottoms, which took considerable time to drain. Since in cold weather this was a daily preflight requirement, much time was saved by installing a quick-drain valve in the tanks so that draining required only a flick of the wrist.

In another improvement, the door was redesigned to allow it to swing up under the wing. The front seat was rebuilt so that it hinged and allowed easier access to the rear. The baggage compartment was extended toward the tail, creating an additional two and a half feet of cargo space. Another important change was made by extending the pilot's window two and a half inches at the wing root, allowing greater visibility when looking for lost people. The difficulty of keeping warm in small planes was solved by installing rear-seat heaters.

Gasoline tanks were completely modified to reduce the risk of condensation, and their necks were extended. Landing on skis was sometimes rougher than outside fuel gauges were built to stand, so they were moved inside.

It was discovered that in winter fine snow would sometimes enter the fuselage through the openings, and would collect to the point of interfering with the control cables. Since the snow was nearly impossible to remove in field conditions, a small trapdoor was installed to allow the removal of the snow before it froze.

With our lives on the line every time we run into a problem, you can see why changes were made to prevent as many problems as possible from occurring. Water in the gasoline of your car is a nuisance; in a plane, it is a really serious problem. Quick-drain visible-sediment bulbs were installed at low places in the fuel line, allowing water to be removed daily if it was present. In the backcountry, an overnight stay in winter meant draining the oil at night. Before it could be replaced in the plane, it had to be heated; this was done more quickly with an extended oil drain. Cold-weather starting was further facilitated by installing stepped-up magnetos. In the early days, condensation was really the warden pilot's nemesis—everything from gasoline, oil, and even the windshield is susceptible in cold weather. The warden pilots managed to solve the windshield problem by installing special defrosters.

Perhaps the most significant of redesign achievements were the skis used on the first warden planes. Factory air skis were generally rigid and known to break on landings. Once again, the wardens went to work, and soon came up with a much better design. Their new ski was made of wood with a metal covering, flexible enough to ride up easily on snow, and not so prone to breakage. Measuring about one foot wide and five feet, eight inches in length, the new ski had greater flotation as well. Reinforcing the structural members where the skis attached finished the job of outfitting their planes to contend with the varying conditions encountered in landings and takeoffs.

It is extremely evident that Maine's flying wardens contributed greatly in the development of the light airplanes that were used by bush pilots everywhere.

In the early 1950s, warden pilots spent most of their time each winter checking beaver trappers in the backcountry. The beaver population had exploded in the 1940s; their pelts were bringing good money, and the interest in trapping beaver was high. Wherever this occurs, there will be poaching problems. Mac Maheu recalls that there were trappers and camps all over the place. Wardens were usually dropped off in an area to work, and were picked up several days later if everything went well. Sometimes it did not; more than a few wardens had to hole up for a few days, waiting for a storm or blow to pass so that the pilot could return. Sometimes the trapper's line was miles long, and the warden could not get back on the designated day. Radio communication was still in the future for the pilots. With no communication, the pilot would tend to become apprehensive about the missing warden, and he would go looking for him. We seem to take radios for granted now, having forgotten the days when wardens worked without them.

It was not at all uncommon for a pilot to be forced down by weather and have to wait out a storm in some remote trapper's camp. On several occasions, these stays lasted for several days and caused great concern on the home fronts. More than once, searches were begun, and newspapers carried stories of missing wardens and pilots. George Later recalls with a grin that it does not take long to acquire a distaste for dried macaroni, which he once ate for several days while holed up in a camp.

Another fairly common occurrence was non-warden lightplanes going down. Since World War II, the number of lightplanes had increased rapidly. Many young men who had been exposed to flying in the service were returning home and buying planes. Now there were trappers, hunters, and fishermen everywhere in lightplanes. Some of them were relatively inexperienced, and their planes were not always equipped in the proper manner. "I swear, sometimes it seemed as though there was at least one down per week. We spent an awful lot of time for a few years looking for downed airplanes," recalls Maheu.

Lost hunters were probably the first people (other than regular wardens) to benefit from our flight capabilities. With very few roads then in the backcountry, hunters could really get lost—many did—and some of them unquestionably owe their lives to warden pilots. Usually taking off just before dawn, a flying warden looks for a telltale wisp of smoke. If he waits very long after daylight, the lost hunter will probably have left his fire to continue on. Therefore, it is critical to see the smoke early and direct a ground warden to the area. (This is easy now with walkie-talkie radios. In the pre-radio days, it meant landing to notify the nearest warden as to the area and compass bearing of the lost man; then, after locating him again, the pilot would either circle him until help arrived or hope he would understand the wing waggles and head in the right direction.)

Many times, unfortunately, especially in November, the cold weather becomes a factor in the survivability of a lost man. Several have been found unable to move and nearly dead from exposure.

Retired Chief Pilot George Later recalls one such incident. A lost lobster fisherman had been the object of a seven-day search. Most of the searchers, save for a few flying wardens, had quit the search and returned home. Finally, George saw a man on his back waving an arm. He made a tight turn and swooped very low to have a look at him. As quickly as possible, he landed and told wardens where the subject was. When wardens got to him, he was nearly done in from hunger, walking, and exposure. As he was being helped from the woods, still wearing his high rubber fishing boots, he related a story: His compass, he said, had been lost the first day, and he had soon lost his bearings. The man was taken to a camp on Lambert Lake. When wardens helped him pull off his boots, his compass fell out.

When George arrived at the camp some time later, the lost man looked up, pointed a finger, and said, "That's the pilot." George grins when he tells the story. "Guess I was low enough on that pass."

Mac Maheu was once flying, looking for a lost New Jersey hunter. The man had been staying at a camp at St. Croix Lake. As sometimes happens, he had been lost for several days before the incident was reported to the wardens. They spotted a dead moose; tracks indicated that the lost man had shot the moose and eaten some meat, then wandered away. His tracks soon disappeared, and he was never found.

Here's another of Mac's oft-told stories—a good one, I think you will agree.

Some out-of-state hunters were staying at camps on Eagle Lake. Prior to leaving for the woods, their guide took them out in the yard and gave them a crash course on compass use. He told them that the needle would bring them back to camp; when they wanted to return, they merely had to follow it. By sheer bad luck, one of the men noticed that, as the guide spoke, the needle was, in fact, pointing at the camp. He became an instant believer. He was finally located three days later still headed north, following the needle. "Christ," Mac says, "he'd have gone clear to Frenchville if we hadn't caught up with him."

One thing that has always impressed me on lost-hunter searches about these flying pilots is their super-keen eyesight and ability to quickly spot things on the ground. As a result of untold hours of low flying while searching for someone, they develop this extra-keen perceptivity. I will never forget circling over my first lost man: At first, I could not see him. When I finally did, I could not believe how small he looked, even at treetop level.

Probably the most significant change in regard to finding lost hunters from airplanes was when it became required that hunters wear an article of fluorescent-orange clothing. This was a tremendous boon to spotting those infinitesimal lost individuals—pilots all agree on the impact of this one new element. International orange, in my opinion, has to be the most unnatural, obnoxious color human eyes will ever see, but this is what makes it stand out from the soft colors of nature.

Retired Chief Pilot Andy Stinson tells of once seeing something move along the edge of a distant bog. He watched as he approached, and soon discovered that it was a hunter wearing a fluorescent-orange cap. His map indicated the distance to have been nearly ten miles from where he first noticed it. Fluorescent orange draws a lot of growls from hunters, but not from warden pilots. There is no doubt that it has saved many lives on land and at sea.

We have discovered one interesting phenomenon of lost people—their will to survive. Therefore, all pilots agree: Don't give up on your man. Many persons have been found after surviving for several days in weather that one could easily assume had done them in. Therefore, a pilot searching for a lost person must steadfastly assume that his subject is alive and trying his damnedest to stay that way, and keep on looking.

The warden pilot's job was, and still is, a risky business. Even with the tremendous improvements to the early planes by pilots like Bill Turgeon, Sleepy Atkins, George Later, and Mac Maheu, there were still pitfalls. Frozen oil lines, clogged breather pipes, and gusty crosswinds were only a few of the difficulties they had to contend with. Even Bill Turgeon was not immune, and once got a broken leg when he caught a wing while landing on Big Wood Lake in Jackman.

From time to time, the early pilots were the victims of plane malfunctions or mishaps, and had to make emergency landings. When this happened, it was not uncommon for the landing to be somewhat less than perfect. Mac Maheu once had a "close encounter" on Nollesemic Lake. After securing a twenty-foot Old Town canoe to the floats, he (and the biologist he had picked up) took off. Shortly after takeoff, a loud snap was heard. It was not apparent for a few moments what had happened. Suddenly a gust of wind hit the plane, and it became all too apparent: One of the stretch-cords holding down the canoe had come unfastened, and the back of the canoe had lifted against the tail, practically immobilizing the rudder. To further complicate matters, the bow swung over into the propeller—and, in an instant, the twenty-foot canoe had become an eighteen-foot canoe. Mac would not say so, but you can be sure it took a calm mind and steady hand to turn a very unresponsive airplane around and put her safely back on the water. "The prop didn't look too hot," says Mac. "With an ax and two flat rocks, I pounded out the prop tips and flew her back to Greenville."

Mac has some other stories. "One winter, I swear, I walked more than I flew. Did you ever climb down a tree you didn't climb up? It's really quite an experience.

"Once I was returning from Waterville to Fort Kent. I didn't follow my normal route because I wanted to check a trapper's camp for activity. I was six or seven miles beyond First Musquacook Lake when oil suddenly began to appear on the windshield. I was on wheels, and I thought I could get back to the lake. I knew the ice was very thin and would be thickest near shore; I hoped to put her down next to the trapper's camp, if I could.

"When the weight of the airplane came onto the ice as she slowed, one wheel broke through, and the plane flipped over on her back. She slowly broke through, and sunk by the nose. At that point, I was sitting on the tail, dreading the wet, icy trip to shore.

"Finally, I started breaking ice, and by keeping my elbows on the edge, I made shore and the camp. There wasn't much food in the camp except some sardines—which I've never eaten since, by the way. There was no ax, either. I remembered that my ax was still under the seat in the plane. As much as I hated to, I went back out and dove down, but couldn't find it; it must have fallen out the door when I left the plane. That wasn't a very comfortable night, I can tell you.

"The next day, I started down the lakeshore in the direction of Ashland. That night I stayed in another camp and called out on a woods telephone. Sleepy Atkins picked me up walking on the road the next day.

"One other time, my engine quit, and I tried to set the plane down on an old road. At the last minute, a gust of wind put me into the trees upside down. I was lucky that time—I only had to walk seven miles," Mac says with a chuckle.

Retired warden Leonard Pelletier was returning to his district by plane late in the afternoon of January 25, 1945. The pilot was a chap named Alexander who had flown briefly for the Warden Service. It was cold and windy, with blowing snow. Suddenly the engine began knocking badly, and they had to put down quickly. This they managed to do on a small flowage.

"It was getting dark fast," Leonard recalls, "and we were a considerable distance from where I knew some lumber camps to be. We struck off on foot in that direction. Soon, we came upon some snowshoe floats. The question was, were they made by someone leaving or going to camp? By luck, we made the right choice, and spent the night at the camps.

"Later, to rescue the plane, we swamped a path through the woods at the edge of the flowage. This was no small job, but we finally packed down 350 feet of snow for a runway, plus the swamping job, to give us about 800 feet for takeoff. Bill Turgeon, Cash Austin, and I carried the ailing engine on a stretcher to another plane. It was taken to be repaired, and brought back. After we carried it back to the plane, we reinstalled it and flew the plane out." Leonard makes this sound almost matter-of-fact, but I suspect it was quite a chore.

During those years, several wardens learned to fly and were called upon to fill vacancies in the warden pilot ranks. One such warden was Earl Kelley. When Sleepy Atkins left flying to become a supervisor, Earl flew in his place. No stories about warden pilots are complete without Earl's classic about Warden Cassius "Cash" Austin. You should really hear Earl tell it, for full effect, but I'll do my best.

First of all, you should know that Cash Austin attained almost legendary status as a game warden in the North Country. Although only five feet, six inches tall, he was built like a small bulldozer and was all business. His exploits and, shall we say, "direct approach," are remembered by many till this day.

The plan was simply to land on Cross Lake and let Cash off at his camp. Earl landed, and taxied toward the camp. A stiff breeze was blowing toward the shore, and there were rocks in the area where Cash was to be dropped off. "Not wishing to damage the floats," Earl says, "I swung the plane around and, keeping only light power on, let her drift tail-first to where Cash could get off. Finally, he said 'Okay,' and got out. I waited a few seconds, then turned the power on and pulled away. There was quite a chop on the water, and I was quickly up to takeoff speed.

"For several seconds I had been hearing a tapping noise, which I thought was probably made by the safety belt shut outside when the door closed. Suddenly, just as I was about to lift off, I glanced over and observed a pair of knuckles at the window. I quickly killed the power. At this point, the grayest, wettest, most bug-eyed face I ever saw appeared at the window. Quickly I opened the door, and Cash got in. 'Christ, I thought you got off,' I said. He didn't speak to me after that for three months."

As the quality and performance of lightplanes continued to

grow, so did the ranks of warden pilots. In 1949, a plane base was established at Eagle Lake. This was followed by a headquarters base and hangar at Greenville in 1952. Other bases were established at Maranacook Lake, Cold Stream Pond, and Rangeley.

In 1955, a step up to bigger planes was recommended, and we purchased a Cessna 180. These bigger planes were tremendous, and for several years were the most utilized of all our models. Their speed and load capacity were far superior to those of the Cubs and the Super Cubs.

Warden pilots were kept extremely busy during the 1950s. Many biological programs required aircraft to transport men and equipment to various places, and many hours were flown for this cause. Pilots who flew in those years recall numerous occasions of flying sports celebrities, famous newscasters, or well-known writers to backcountry locations. The Fish and Game Department was expanding by leaps and bounds, and these were good promotional tactics.

One particular group, however, did not make out too well. Several members of the Governor's Council were once flown by warden aircraft to Desolation Pond on a fishing trip. It was politely suggested upon their arrival that they comply with the existing regulations regarding the bag limit. However, they were visited by district warden Bill Vernon, and several of the men received summonses for being in violation of that very regulation. This had much the same effect as that of a small bomb. Predictably, there were reverberations, but the Warden Service did not back down one inch. For some reason, this just tickles the hell out of me. Wardens who can remember the incident agree that if nothing else, it established and promoted the fact that wardens are fair, and make no differentiation between the big guy and the little guy in such cases.

By now, airplanes had become an important part of a warden's life, with nearly every aspect enhanced by their presence. Most wardens like to fly, and do so fairly regularly; some, however, get airsick, and, from a pilot's point of view, make somewhat less-than-desirable passengers. One warden once told me that even the sound of an electric fan made him sick.

My first plane trip as a warden cured me. It was shortly after daylight when pilot Andy Stinson and I took off from Meddybemps Lake to look for some overdue duck hunters on the Dennys River. The Dennys River is so crooked, I am not even sure it runs downhill. For about forty-five minutes, we followed its course down and back, not far over the trees. I could not see straight for two days after, but I did not get sick. It sure was a pleasure, though, to get out when we landed. Since then, I have never even burped while flying. It has been over twenty years, and I cannot remember where the duck hunters showed up, but I remember the ride. It is strange how some people are affected by flight, and others not. As I write this, I am thinking of one warden who, if he reads this, will be feeling queasy already.

If you fly, you will undoubtedly have some experiences that stand out in your mind.

Late in the afternoon on a pleasant winter day, Andy Stinson, Leonard Ritchie, and myself were en route back to Indian Lake in Whiting. About a mile ahead, a jet fighter crossed our path at about the same altitude. We watched him until he nearly disappeared, then noticed another some distance behind. He, too, crossed our path, but we were much closer to this one. Suddenly, Leonard hollered, "Watch it." A third fighter was coming in our direction nearly off our right wing. Andy pulled the Cessna into a steep climb for a few seconds. We pitched down in time to see him pass by, and he was close enough that we could see his white helmet. If he had glanced to the left, he might have seen three white faces. No one spoke for a few seconds. Finally, Leonard broke the tension. "It is a good thing we didn't hit him," he said. "We'd have cut him right in two."

Warden Pilot Jack McPhee, who flies the northern part of Maine, is constantly on the watch for military aircraft that take advantage of the remoteness there for training maneuvers. In one instance, he recalls, while flying his patrol, the sky directly over-head was suddenly full of B-52 bombers. This sure would perk up a guy's day, now, wouldn't it? As you know by now, warden pilots are sometimes involved in rescuing stranded or injured people, and often must contend with hazardous circumstances. The following incident, I think, exemplifies the spirit and courage and skill of warden pilots better than any I know.

Late in the afternoon of February 11, 1974, warden pilot Gary Dumond landed on Spider Lake to spend the night at pilot Jack McPhee's camp. They were settled in for the evening (they thought) when, around eight p.m., another camp owner arrived and reported that two men had been badly injured in a snowmo-bile accident. It was a black night with light snow falling. Two men on a snowmobile had struck the end of a rocky point in the lake while traveling very fast. Both were unconscious and bleeding. As quickly as possible, both planes were made ready; all the seats except the pilots' were removed, and the planes taxied to the scene. Each unconscious man was loaded into a plane, along with some-one to attend him. Then, with snow still falling and in the dark, they prepared to take off.

Gary got off fine. Jack nearly did not. Luckily, he saw the island looming up on him just as he lifted off. In a tight maneuver to avoid it, he dragged the right wingtip in the snow and kept going.

Their destination was the Presque Isle Airport. At one point, the victim in Jack's plane partially came to and began grabbing wildly at things. He managed to yank some wires loose before being calmed down. Finally, both planes landed, and the victims were transported by ambulance. It is during times like these that you earn your money.

The value of helicopters in law enforcement efforts has long been recognized. They are an extremely useful tool in many aspects of fish and game work, as well. Therefore, when several became available through government surplus, the Maine Warden Service eagerly obtained some and put them to good use. Several of the younger pilots had learned to fly helicopters in the military; Gary Dumond and Dana Toothaker had seen duty in Vietnam. In fact, Dana, who later became chief pilot, was assigned as Vice President Agnew's pilot when he toured Vietnam.

These first helicopters were two-place Bells, and were very underpowered. It was not uncommon on hot days for them to be unable to take off with a passenger on board. Later on, several with more power were acquired and proved very satisfactory. Each year, many hours were being spent on dog-deer problems in southern and central Maine, as well as on lost hunters, and it was on these searches that the helicopters became invaluable. Men and equipment could be moved very quickly to any place, no matter how remote.

One incident involving helicopters and their capabilities stands out in my mind. Two canoeists had tried to run Big Ambejackmockamus Falls on the West Branch of the Penobscot

River below Ripogenus Dam, but had upset, and one of them had drowned. Dana and I were searching the river below the dam from a helicopter. In some white water I noticed something appear from time to time, then disappear. Upon taking a closer look, I decided that it was a piece of dark-colored clothing, but after I watched it appear and disappear several times, I did not believe the victim was there. I mentioned to Dana that I would like to have the garment to see if the survivor could identify it as the victim's.

Slowly, he maneuvered the helicopter down until the float-tips were touching the water, and held it there. I crawled out and, by lying on the float, grabbed the garment and retrieved it. This took several seconds, during which Dana held the ship stationary, still touching the rushing white water. I was impressed. The shirt was indeed the victim's, and shortly afterward we located the body in a pool farther downriver. After we notified the others, Dana landed until some divers had secured the body to a float, and he brought it out.

This is but one example of the various jobs helicopters are able to perform. George Later planted the first Atlantic salmon in the Penobscot River with a helicopter. Most good things, however, do not last forever, and this includes helicopters. Although we found them to be very useful pieces of equipment, especially for search and rescue, they were apparently too expensive to maintain, and their use in the Maine Warden Service was discontinued.

The enthusiasm and dedication generated by the early pilots have been handed down over the years to those who followed. Even though the number of pilots and planes has been sadly reduced, and several plane bases discontinued because of financial problems, those that remain carry on in the finest tradition. Aircraft continue to be the good right arm of the Maine Warden Service.

11 — THE WARDENS' WIVES

If you are not or have never been a game warden's wife, you have probably never had much reason to think about what it must be like. Many years ago, two wardens' wives wrote books about their lives in the wilderness of northern Maine. The two women, Helen Hamlin and Annette Jackson, both wrote fine stories concerning their husbands' jobs and experiences. They spoke of being alone for days on end while the men were off on snowshoes or patrolling their districts by canoe. These wives frequently went on patrol with their men, and had a genuine interest in and understanding of exactly what it was that a warden did.

A warden's wife of long ago almost always lived in a primitive warden camp, and had to make of it the best home she could. A warden's pay was quite meager in those days, and many a warden had accepted the job for less money than he had earned on his previous job. These wages certainly did not allow the purchase of nice furniture or other household items. Many camps, in fact, had only the furniture made by the warden, or maybe his predecessor. In those days it required, I suspect, more dedication to be a warden's wife than it did to be a warden.

Many women would not be at all comfortable in the role of

a warden's wife. I have mentioned elsewhere that being a warden is more a way of life than a job. Then it is quite reasonable, I think, to say that the warden's wife is engulfed—and that may be a poor choice of words—in her husband's career as few other women are.

When a woman marries a game warden, I suspect she must initially suffer a reaction that borders on culture shock. I am not joking, either. Consider this: I once knew a young game warden whose wife grew up in Portland. When he met her, she had never even heard of a game warden. The next thing she knew, she was living in a one-room log camp on the thoroughfare between Chamberlain Lake and Round Pond. The camp was equipped with such conveniences as an outhouse and a hand pump for water. Period. This particular girl, however, took it all in stride, and whenever a difficulty or setback arose, she would just grin and make the best of it. Every once in a while, though, her city origins shone through.

I was her husband's sergeant and used to work with him quite frequently. One morning after I arrived, we were having a cup of coffee before he and I left for the day. "Could you get me some red paint?" she asked. "What in the world do you want with red paint?" I replied. "Well," she said, "on nice days I like to sun myself on the dock, and it's so drab-looking." I laughed, and told her I did not think a red dock would mesh with the decor of the Allagash Wilderness Waterway, which went right by the door.

Many wardens and their wives start out in the remote districts, then move "out" to civilization as their children become school-aged. It is then that sometimes the woods don't seem so bad, after all—at least, in the woods, you have some privacy. This is lost to some degree once the move is made to farther south in Maine, where it becomes more hectic for a warden's wife as well as for the warden himself.

A game warden's home is essentially his headquarters. He goes about his business at all hours of the day and night, and his wife in effect runs the office in his absence. Most people have a place of employment where they go to work, leaving it behind when they come home; this is not the case with us. If someone has a question or message for the warden, they'll make a phone call or go to his house to see him. During busy times, housework is something a warden's wife tries to work in between taking phone calls and messages for the warden. Some wives can answer fish-and-game-law questions on a level equal to their husbands. This sure is helpful for the warden, but it does not do much for his wife's day.

One inconvenience shared by game wardens is hardly ever being home at mealtimes—or being whisked away on some emergency. I've never understood what natural law causes a warden to miss so damned many suppertimes. It is just one of those things that has to be, I guess. As bad as it seems for the warden, it must be a whole lot worse for the woman who prepared the supper that, by traditional Yankee standards, is the main get-together, talk-it-over part of the day. This happens routinely year in, year out, for wardens' wives, and I can only hope they understand. Most do come to accept it as part of the role of being married to a man whose comings and goings are usually in no way clock–oriented, but more in similarity with the Indians, whose activities were affected only by the changes in the seasons.

Yes, indeed, the sudden change from being a housewife to being a member of the law enforcement community can have some interesting side effects. Sometimes these side effects are of a subtle nature; other times, not so subtle.

Many a new warden and his family, upon moving to their first location, quickly learn that things are not the same anymore.

The young warden spends his hours away from home, learning his new district and meeting people. He soon understands that he is viewed very differently than he was before putting on the uniform. His wife, on the other hand, has the job of maintaining the home and trying to settle into community life. It is here that sometimes a social snag is struck. Her role has changed, too. Whether she likes it or not, she is married to the man whom many people in her new community have learned to "watch out for." She may notice things, such as conversations that quickly subside when she enters a place of business, or when the people she meets in the store suddenly seem to be engrossed in something else and not notice her.

In one case I know of, a young warden's wife got a job in a store. One day, a man came in to buy some pants. While she waited on him, they talked. The conversation was of a routine nature; he said he had not seen her before, and asked where she lived. It happened that he lived in the same nearby small town. He could not seem to recall the house she described, so she told him she was the warden's wife. He reacted by throwing the pants on the counter and walking out. The reaction was maybe not a typical one, but the message was very clear. Granted, this is an extreme case, but it certainly serves to illustrate the lower mentality some people are blessed with.

Another aspect dealt with by warden families from time to time involves the children. Usually, children get along fairly well with each other, no matter who they are. However, you can be sure that at some point a warden's school-aged son will come home in tears, and tell his mother that some boys pounded on him because "your father pinched my father" for something or other. Try explaining this to a young wife and mother.

However trying the first few years may seem to a warden's

wife, it all gets better as time goes on. Kids grow up, and the jagged-edged problems seem less so as time rounds off the corners. Still, it takes a strong, tolerant woman to be married to a game warden. She learns to accept not having weekends off to go here and there like other folks do. She may go with the children or with friends, but she will seldom be there with her husband. For myself, I can recall having to miss many school functions involving my children that conflicted with the job I was being paid to do. Consequently, my wife went alone. This has always been, I am sure, a constant burden, and sometimes a source of aggravation for wardens' wives.

Many times, I have heard someone say to my wife, "Oh, it must be fun being a warden's wife, bringing up all those cute baby animals." I do not know if it can actually be called fun; it would seem to be, rather, just one more occupational hazard. It is not uncommon, however, for a warden to return home and be greeted by his wife or kids with, "Guess what we've got now?" It gets so that you hardly dare ask "What?" anymore.

You would not believe some of the things people bring. Luckily, most wardens' wives are accommodating, and develop a knack for providing adequate temporary care for an injured this or apparently abandoned that. I am sure my wife's experiences are no different from those of other wardens' wives. The various creatures she has cared for include deer fawns, bear cubs, tiny beaver kits, foxes, rabbits, turtles, sparrows, hawks, saw-whet owls, raccoons, woodchucks, skunks, crows, seagulls, and probably others that I cannot remember. (In fact, there are some I have tried to forget. These include the seagulls and all those with spike teeth. For some reason, most anything you can name would bite me, if given a chance.) People are forever picking up young wild animals and after attempting to care for them, will usually give up and bring them to the warden. I am sure most wardens' wives would agree that the role of surrogate mother to some wild animal, even if brief, can be time-consuming as well as hectic. Luckily, the larger foundlings, like deer and bear, enjoy only a short stay until arrangements can be made to transfer them to the state Game Farm, where they can be cared for by full-time professionals.

I hope I have painted a fairly accurate picture of the important role that game wardens' wives play in their husbands' careers. The bottom line is this: The occupation of being a game warden's wife, and how well a woman can adjust to it, seems to have a direct bearing on the effort her husband puts into his job. Her role is often many-fold. Along with being a mother and a housewife, she is in fact an unsung, unpaid, but in no way unappreciated game warden's assistant. That will get a lot of cheers from wardens' wives everywhere, and it is absolutely true.

I would like to end this chapter with a poem written many years ago by Lyla St. Louis, whose father, Lyle Smith, was warden at Mount Desert for a long time. She seems to capture the feeling of what it is like being a warden's wife, probably better than I have been able to convey. She kindly allowed me to use her poem, and I deeply appreciate it.

The Game Warden's Wife

Some people think that a warden's life
Is an easy, carefree one.
But what about the warden's wife,
Do you think she has fun?

She works each day from dawn 'til dark,
Her work is never done.
She goes upstairs to make the beds—
Ding-a-ling! The doorbell's rung.

She hurries quickly down the stairs,
And rushes to the door.
"Is the warden in?" a stranger asks;
"Oh, he won't be in till four."

Then back she goes about her work,
She starts to make a cake.
The telephone rings, ding-a-ling,
"No, he won't be home till late."

The whole day long she's back and forth
From door to telephone.
I wonder how she carries on
The spirit of home sweet home.

She spends the frosty nights alone,
But soon gets used to that.
At least she doesn't have to have
Those cold feet in her back.

She's up all hours of the night,
She's lost all trace of fear.
A stranger standing at the door
Says, "I've just struck a deer."

"Did you cut his throat?" she promptly asks,
Then grabs the butcher knife.
"If you haven't, I can do that too;
It's nothing in my life."

So if you think the warden's wife
Can live a life that's grand,
Just change with her a day or two,
And then you'll understand.

12 — ALL IN A DAY'S WORK—AT NIGHT

To say that some things are as different as night and day, from a warden's point of view, is an understatement—and you soon learn, when becoming a game warden, just how much of an understatement.

A goodly portion of your work is performed at night, because much of the activity involved in the illegal taking of fish or game—like any other illegal activity—takes place under the cover of darkness.

Another trend you soon catch on to is that of "things going bump in the night." Murphy, the same chap who compiled Murphy's Laws, surely spent his training period going about the countryside, creating hazards for wardens to encounter in the dark. I am referring specifically to old clotheslines, old pieces of farm equipment long abandoned in some field, boulders hidden in the grass, old cellar holes, etc. You can begin to get the picture. I know of no warden who hasn't discovered several of these occupational hazards the same way I did—the hard way. These obstacles can be harmful to your health as well as to your vehicle. If you are inclined to be uncomfortable (a polite word for afraid) in the dark, a game warden's life is definitely not for you.

Many occupations require going to work in the evening hours. Most of those jobs, however, are performed with some sort of artificial lighting. The very nature of warden's night work means you must get about without the use of a light, which would give away your location or make your presence known. It is really very simple: To apprehend someone who is poaching fish or game in the dark, you must get very close, very quietly, and observe his activities prior to the actual arrest. The objective may be simple, but it's achieving it that frequently is not.

I do not know of any type of job that gives more insight into how people act in the dark while being unknowingly observed. Believe me, many people's behavior is substantially different, and often not for the better.

Many animals that seem so elusive during the day are also most active in darkness. In fact, this is true for the most part with all wildlife. This is when they become most vulnerable to predators—including man—and so wardens sit and watch and wait. After spending hundreds of hours in darkness, you acquire a great deal of awareness in regard to these animals and their nocturnal activities. It is a unique experience that few, other than game wardens, ever come to experience, and most do not even suspect exists.

For example, it is not uncommon for deer to walk up to your vehicle and sniff it. Sometimes they become alarmed and stamp their front feet before wandering off. You can lure a distant owl to a nearby tree by squeaking like a small injured animal. The woods and fields that seem so barren during the day literally come alive at night, and quite often provide some entertainment for a warden on his long nightly vigils. Darkness and moving about in it become second nature for wardens. A good flashlight is not a convenience;

it is an absolute necessity. A warden would sooner leave home without his boots than without a flashlight. Much of the work requires operating in darkness, but at some critical points, a good light is a must.

I think you will understand more about things that go bump in the night after reading about several wardens' experiences.

My own first such encounter came, as you may recall, early in my career and involved a wire clothesline under the nose taken at full speed. This was a very educational experience for me, and I have envied short game wardens ever since. I have even acquired a style of running similar to that of Groucho Marx. It works well, except on barbed-wire fences. (They are hell, believe me.)

The second encounter occurred one dark night when my partner Elmer Knowlton and I were working our way toward some illegal fishermen on the thoroughfare at Sourdnahunk Lake. I walked my face right into a ten-inch-diameter post. I knew it was there, too; l just did not know where. Hell of a way to find it! You may wonder how a person with my luck ever survived this long.

Working the spring smelt runs has traditionally provided some unique experiences, not only for wardens, but for smelters, as well. This activity occurs in the early spring when everyone, wardens included, is ready for some action after a long winter. Smelting appears to be some sort of psychological rite in which people are compelled to flock in droves to the same spot where they can get drunk, whoop and holler, or fall in the ice water, all for a little pail of smelts. You add the darkness factor, and some mighty interesting things can and do happen.

Years ago, Elmer Knowlton and another warden crept up on two figures dipping smelts in a closed brook. When they made the rush, the subjects fled across the brook. Elmer jumped on the back of one, who continued on across the brook and up the far bank before collapsing under the weight. "You know," Elmer said, "that had to be the strongest woman I ever saw."

Sometimes darkness can work for you. Take, for instance, one night when wardens Mickey Noble and Eben Perry were at Indian Rock on Kennebago Stream. They stood in the shadows and watched the comings and goings of several hundred smelters. A man came along and, under his breath, asked if they had seen any wardens around. "We did a little while ago," they said. "Well, look," the man said, "I've got some extra smelts here. I'll give them to you, if you want them." "We'll take them," said Mickey.

Usually, though, darkness is the villain. One night, warden Jim Davis and I were working a closed brook. We were in the process of issuing summonses to a party who had come along and dipped in a small pool where the smelts had collected. Meanwhile, another group of young men came along on their way to the lake, which was open to smelting. When the group being summonsed left, we returned to our position of concealment near the pool. In a few minutes, the second group returned. For several minutes they watched the smelts in the pool. We could hear some conversation about whether we were still in the area. Finally, they moved on up the trail.

A few seconds later, we heard running footsteps coming back to the pool, and shortly thereafter we heard the sound of a net being raked along the gravel bottom. In about four jumps, we were at the top of the bank beside the pool. "Hold it right there," I said as we snapped on the flashlights. Down over the bank beside the water was one of the teenagers with a small tree limb in his hands. "What do you think you are doing?" I asked. "Oh, nothing," he said, "just washing off this branch." I quickly told him I thought the branch was clean by now and he had best head on up the trail. "Yes, sir," he said, grinning, and took off. We had to laugh at being suckered out by a kid.

As you can see, things that happen in the dark are not always what they seem to be. One warden tells of the night he crept to a spot on a closed brook where he had reason to believe subjects would be taking smelts to keep alive for bait. He crept close to the brook and could hear voices. In the dark he finally was able to make out the silhouettes of two men sitting side by side on the bank. Quietly, he made his way to where he could rush the two. He quickly made his move, and suddenly discovered he had captured two forty-quart steel milk cans.

In another instance, Lieutenant Bill Vernon recalls working the Long Lake smelt run. Subjects were heard approaching the mouth of the brook. No lights were seen, but the clink of nets and pails could be heard. The rush was made upon one very startled escaped cow dragging her chain.

It is not uncommon for these same animals that we try to protect to create humorous situations from time to time. Mike Pratt was on foot one night in a back field. He had received complaints of someone on foot night-hunting a series of fields. This particular night, it was raining hard. After a couple hours of watching and waiting, he thought he heard something. Sure enough, a man was approaching his location. He could hear his legs as they swished through the grass. A thin rick of bushes dividing two fields separated Mike and the foot-jacker. Always hoping for the element of surprise, Mike waited for the right moment to make his move. Hoping his rush would intersect the night hunter's path, he jumped from the bushes, snapped his light on the subject, and yelled, "Hold it." But he never got the words "game warden" out. "There, just ten feet from me, stood a bull moose, big as all outdoors. We both left quickly in opposite directions." That sure would perk up an otherwise dull evening, now, wouldn't it?

Leon Wilson had a similar experience many years ago. While on his way home late one evening, he thought he caught a glimpse of something in a field under an apple tree. He continued down the road some distance, then pulled off and quietly walked back. Sure enough, in the gloom he could make out a man under an apple tree some distance off. Suspecting a night hunter, he carefully worked his way around the field in the shadows. Then, like Mike Pratt, he made his rush and snapped his light on a bear, which promptly reared up on its hind legs. I asked him, Did the bear run, or what? "I don't really know if he ran or not," Leon chuckled. "I didn't look back to see."

Several times while I have been sitting out at night, small animals like mice and shrews have run across my legs. Warden Phil Dumond once had this unique experience: "I had taken my sleeping bag and walked quite some distance to watch a natural salt lick at the edge of a blueberry field along the boundary. Several deer had been shot there recently. It was a cold, frosty fall night, so I sat in my sleeping bag for several hours. Sometime after midnight, I decided that no one would come this late, so I got ready to leave. But it was a long way home, so I decided to sleep right there. I crawled back into my sleeping bag and went to sleep. At some point, I was awakened by something heavy on top of me. At first I thought it was a bear. As I scrambled to get out of the sleeping bag, I found that there were branches and bushes around my face. Finally, it dawned on me: Somehow I had laid my sleeping bag in a beaver's run. How he failed to notice me, I don't know, but he soon came back and crawled right over me, dragging a small tree back to the water. I wasn't too sleepy after that."

There are, as you can see, many different things that can happen to one whose occupation requires him to go continuously moving about in the darkness, trying to convince himself he can see. Sometimes the bumps are real bumps. I shudder to think of how many a warden has wound up in a ditch or astraddle some rock, trying his damnedest to get from his position of concealment out to the road without giving himself or his position away by turning on his lights.

Most wardens are extremely familiar with places where they work most often, and know how to come and go even on the blackest nights. It is usually the unfamiliar ones that get you.

On one occasion, Warden Elmer Knowlton and myself were on our way home from the Ripogenus Dam area. It was in the early morning hours. Suddenly, headlights appeared behind me, although quite some distance back. I quickly began to look for a place to duck off and let whoever-it-was pass without recognizing my vehicle. I swung off into a small gap and doused my lights. Wanting to make sure I was out of sight, I drove in the road a few feet farther—until a loud clanging noise, much like a fan chewing off a stick of wood, was heard. A large limb had split off an elm tree and had landed in the road, with a long spear thrust outward. This I had managed to impale my radiator on. Elmer was real proud. We drove like hell for Millinocket, stopping at every brook, where we would each grab one of my spare rubber boots, fill it with water, pour it in the radiator, then drive like hell again. We almost made it, too, but finally the flying water under the hood was just too much, and the engine drowned.

Bumps in the night come in all sizes: Some are big, some

little; some loud, others very subtle. I used to work with a warden named Norman Trask. One night we drove to an area where we suspected night hunters were apt to be. We drove up to the top of a hillside orchard and parked the cruiser at the tree line. From there the road continued, but dropped downhill abruptly. We sat in the vehicle and waited. The plan, if someone drove in, was for Norman to back the car down just over the crest, out of sight.

At some point, we thought we heard a vehicle, so I got out. Norman backed the car down into the woods a ways. No car came, but Norman suddenly reappeared on foot. "Come look," he said. "At what?" I replied. "Never mind, I can't tell you. Just come look." We quickly returned to his vehicle. There it sat, with the rear end hanging out over space. A recent gravel excavation had removed most of the side hill in that area, and the road had been rerouted around the edge. The rear tires were literally one inch from the lip of a thirty-foot drop.

"How come you stopped there?" I asked. "Well, I thought I heard a stick break, so I got out to see," he replied. "But, guess what—I can't find any stick." That is how close it comes, sometimes.

This story continues on, by the way: Possibly due to the sound of a breaking stick that was not there, serious injury or worse was avoided; otherwise, a few years later, Norman might not have become deputy commissioner of Fish and Wildlife. It is a strange thing about that stick.

The most bizarre bump in the night I ever heard of was, unfortunately, one I was personally involved in. This is the nightmarish incident I touched on earlier. It happened many years ago, one night with a bright moon and snow on the ground.

My inspector Bob Thomas had picked me up in his new Ford

cruiser, which he had only had for two days. (Already you are guessing at the outcome of the story.) We proceeded to an area where deer were still coming to paw out frozen apples alongside the road. Once snow comes, it is difficult to park in your favorite places of concealment; the vehicle tracks are a tipoff to your presence. The bright moon on the snow does not enhance your chances much, either.

We finally decided to park in the driveway of a large barn near the apple trees. There were no houses around, and other vehicle tracks were already present from the road to the barn. From time to time, as a vehicle approached, we simply backed into the barn out of sight and got out to watch the vehicle. When it passed, we pulled back out. We did this several times. Finally, a pickup truck came along, and we backed in out of sight. This particular vehicle did not pass. It drove up to the front and stopped. A man got out and, before we could speak to him, began to scream and curse us at the top of his voice about being in his barn. He made it extremely obvious that he was upset, to say the least. We tried to calm him down, but to no avail; it only made him worse. Still screaming and cursing, he climbed onto a large farm tractor that was parked in the barn. He fired it up, and began to rev the engine up and down. There was no muffler, and the noise was deafening. The screaming continued, and the whole thing seemed like a bad dream. We certainly would have left, but the pickup was blocking the entrance.

At this point, he must have decided he did not like the looks of the new Fords. With a scream similar to a "Banzai" attack, he began to demolish the car with the front end of the tractor. He did a good job, too. In the manner of a bull goring a downed matador, he rooted that car all over the barn. Many thoughts raced through my mind, and at least one included shooting him off the tractor. However, two wrongs do not make a right. Because we were in his barn, we decided he was doing all the wrong things all by himself, without us making it worse. Finally, when the car was dead, he left the front of the tractor impaled in the car, and left.

This subject was later taken to court and convicted, plus sued for damages, which he paid. Another bizarre twist of this already-bizarre story was that the judge who heard the case thought it was funny. At the conclusion of the proceedings, he said there was an element of humor involved, and someday we would all see it. I think he was perhaps wrong. I have a fair sense of humor, and, after twenty years, you would think I would have seen it by now if I were ever going to. As for the barn owner, I do not know what caused his reaction. It was certainly apparent that he did not like having game wardens in his barn. You would have to agree that he had a unique way of expressing himself, however.

It goes without saying, I guess, that some things are predictable and some are not. Game wardens the world around share this same occupational hazard, and bumps in the night are predictably unpredictable occurrences for us. Sooner or later, it will be your turn. I hope when your bump in the night comes, it will be a fairly gentle one.

13 — THE ANIMALS

When you make your living by working with various types of fish and game, it is on a rather routine basis that you'll happen upon various and often humorous incidents. In regard to fish, I can only say that they are usually quite well behaved. They never seem to create any problems other than from a law enforcement angle. With animals, however, it is another story. They do fine, as a rule, until somehow they manage to wind up in a place where they do not belong, doing something they are not supposed to do. Then, almost anything can happen. No animal I can think of—in Maine, at least—is entirely reticent. Whether it is a moose or a flying squirrel, you can bet that at some point he will figure out a way to be where he is not welcome.

Without a doubt, a moose, by his sheer size, has to top the list of awkward visitors. When you have a moose problem, you have a problem. Most of the time they are pretty well behaved. It is when fall comes and the bulls go a little haywire that the problems generally occur. With one thing on their minds, they seem to lose all sense, and are just as apt to take a little stroll through town or the schoolyard as not. It is then that the warden gets called.

How do you go about approaching an animal that may

weigh up to half a ton? Very carefully, believe me. Usually, by the time the warden gets there, the local citizenry has gathered; and by then, the moose is not only scared, he is also mad as hell. Parked cars, fences, and clotheslines are often what take the brunt of his wrath before he can be herded out of town. Sometimes, unfortunately, when public safety is involved, the animal has to be put down before he can hurt someone.

In the fall of 1984, one of the wardens in my area received a call that a bull moose had gotten into the canal in Rumford and was being held by the current against the grating where the water left the canal. Along with a sizable crew of volunteers, the warden managed to loop a rope around the moose's horns, and it was then dragged away from the suction. A large front-end loader lifted him up over the steep canal side onto the level, upon which the rope was allowed to slip through his horns until he was free. At this point, the moose jumped back in the water and wound up in the same predicament. The whole process was repeated with one difference: This time, when the moose got free, he wanted to play "I'll get you" for a while before lumbering off.

The only thing you can depend on a moose to do is exactly what you hope he will not do. If you see a moose beside the road, you hope it will not run in front of you; but it will.

Many years ago in East Millinocket, my next-door neighbors were out for an evening drive. They were not even out of town when suddenly a large bull ran directly in front of them. Unable to stop in time, they struck the moose and knocked him down. They sat breathlessly aboard the International Scout, which lurched and rocked while the moose extricated himself from underneath. Eventually, he got to his feet and stood glaring at the vehicle. After several minutes, he walked on down the road. Finally, when they were sure he was gone, they both got out to inspect the damage. Due to a previous problem, the passenger door was not functional, so it meant they both had to get out on the driver's side. As they stood there checking out the vehicle, they heard—then saw in the headlights—the moose coming back at a dead run. In their haste to get back in the same door, they collided and wedged themselves in briefly before they were able to both get in the Scout and slam the door. At this point, the moose made several hooks at the door, leaving some deep gouges. This was too much for the Mrs., and she fainted dead away. This time the moose left and did not come back.

Belligerent seems to be the best word for describing a moose on his worst behavior—which is, in fact, only slightly worse than when he is on his best behavior. I once knew of two railroad employees who were putt-putting along on a small, motorized "Pied," as they are called. As they rounded a curve, they found they were fast approaching a large bull moose standing between the rails. These cars do not stop on a dime, and before the men managed to stop, they had gotten fairly close. At this point, the hair on his hump was bristling, and he charged the car. The men abandoned ship quickly and took off for the woods. The moose proceeded to hook the windshield out, then continued the contest until he had set the car off the rails. He then stalked victoriously off down the tracks.

This may have been a victory for him, but each year a great number of his relatives do not fare so well in their encounters with the railroad. In northern Maine, especially, wardens always respond to several calls per year from the railroad, reporting a moose struck by the train. This occurs year-round. In the winter, if the snow is exceptionally deep, the tracks offer a chance for easier mobility that moose often take advantage of. During blackfly time, they seem to stand around in the open where there might be a breeze and fewer flies. Most collisions occur, however, during the rutting season, when the bulls are traveling and the rails seem made to order for a moose set on taking a hike.

Sometimes a little Yankee ingenuity is all that is needed to get rid of a nuisance moose. Several years ago, a moose had somehow fallen into an old well in the town of Weld. Spectators and wardens alike scratched their heads, trying to come up with a feasible way to perform the extrication. Several ideas were brought forth. Included among them was the suggestion of pumping the water from the well. Mike Pratt, a fairly new game warden in that district, suggested instead, "Let's fill it up with more water." The fire department pumper came, filled the well, and floated the moose to the top—and away he went. Don't you just hate new guys, sometimes?

A moose seems to know only one thing, and that is how to be a moose. This seems to mean: I will go where I want to, when I want, and don't let anything get in the way, or I will knock it down and drag it off. These animals can come completely unglued when something panics them. I once witnessed an incident that illustrates this complete breakdown of what small amount of rationale they may possess.

Early in the spring, Warden Elmer Knowlton and myself were headed for Sourdnahunk Lake from Ripogenus Dam. The road we were on had melted off bare due to its having been plowed for part of the winter. There were snowbanks, however, three or four feet high on both sides. After traveling several miles, we came upon a small bull standing in the road. He had apparently discovered the easy walking, and seemed in no way obliged to get off and let us pass.

As we drew closer, he turned and began a leisurely walk away from us. We followed him for a mile or so, hoping that maybe we'd come to a clearing where he would get off the road. No luck! Finally, we decided that if we could scare him a little, that might work. It didn't.

We decided to drop back and wait. He stood and looked back. At this point, we decided maybe we could pass him. He quickly showed us his speed—which is considerable, by the way, when a moose gallops. When we came to a wide place, we pulled around him and went by. I think I could have slapped his flank as we passed, if I had wanted to—that is how close we were.

Within a few seconds, we were far in front of him. We had gotten about two hundred yards ahead of him, and still he ran, now chasing us. Elmer pulled up, and I got out and stood by the rear of the truck as the moose approached, still galloping. When he was a few yards away, I hollered and waved my arms. This seemed to break the spell, and he turned and galloped back down the road the way he had come. We laughed, and proceeded along.

A minute or two later, I looked back. "Step on it," I hollered, "here he comes again!" Sure enough, he was coming on a dead run, and gaining fast. The impulse to run apparently had shorted out his "which way" mechanism. Yes, sir—when there is a moose involved, you can count on having an interesting diversion.

Bears! The very word causes most game wardens to reach for the Excedrin. Everyone likes bear stories, myself included—and, believe me, bears have provided us with a great many over the years. Most animals that from time to time wind up in our bad graces at least seem to have arrived there by accident, not design. This is not the way it is, however, with bears. You take big and strong, and combine these with cunning and appetite, and you have got yourself a bear. I have always suspected that some animals have acquired a bad reputation that they did not earn or deserve. Believe me, bears have earned theirs.

It is their food-foraging endeavors that generally get them into trouble. Years ago, the lumber camps always had problems with bears raiding the food supplies. Most of the cooks constantly fried in fat, and bears love this. One camp was so plagued by bears that retired warden supervisor Dave Priest once killed five in one night. I am sure this contributed greatly to the peace of mind of the men. (For some reason I have never understood, Canadian woodsmen have a deathly fear of bears. I remember once, when several men were asleep in a camp that had a screen door at each end of the building, they arose in the morning to discover that the lower part of the screening on each door had been wrecked. A bear had pushed his way in one screen and gone out the other. The job lost five men at that very moment—they packed up and left for Canada.)

Bears, of course, have a well-known fondness for honey. Each year, they ruin many hives in their attempts to get at the great-tasting stuff inside. These raids invariably precede a call to the local warden by an irate beekeeper who wants something done.

The first year I was a warden, I received a complaint from a man who stated that a bear had upset his hive and made a shambles of it. He lived by himself in what had been a fairly decent two-story house at one time; now it did not appear to be in much better shape than his one rim-wracked beehive, which was located in a field behind the house. Being new, and lacking experience in such matters, I really did not know what to tell him. However, when he began to tell the local gentry who all gathered at the local store for coffee each morning, they knew what to tell him. With eager ears, he listened to a suggestion that he should repair his hive; then, at dark, leave a lantern lit on top of it to keep the bear away.

That night, the lantern sat burning atop the hive. Not content (as you might suspect) to drop the ball there, one of the men waited until late evening, then snuck up and completely demolished the lantern on a rock. The following morning, the store was a-buzz. "You've had it now," they told him. "That bear burned his paw on that light and it made him so mad, he stove it all to hell. Now he'll go for every light he sees, with a vengeance." This part of the story I was told a couple days later, when I stopped at the store. "If you don't believe it, go see for yourself," the men laughed. I drove up and, sure enough, he had moved everything to the second floor, and all the ground-floor windows were boarded over.

Sometimes bears can be outrageously clever. In the mountains of western Maine, where I live, there are several dairy farms. Each one has several fields in which fodder corn is raised for feed. As soon as it starts to ripen, bears congregate and proceed to wreak havoc on those fields. I have seen a thirty-acre field with at least half the corn laid flat from bears rolling around in it, pulling it down, and just plain raising hell. A neighbor of mine who lives on a farm grinds his corn for grain, some of which he sells. These bags of grain are stored on pallets in a garage that sits right at the edge of the road, directly across from a potato house that has a large mercury-vapor light on the front. From time to time, my neighbor had noticed that a bag of grain was gone, but merely assumed that his wife was selling the corn to local people.

One night, not long after dark, a man stopped and told him there was a bag of grain in the road near the garage. Upon investigating, he found that the eighty-pound bag of corn had been removed from his garage. It was then that he became suspicious and began to look around. He soon discovered what had been happening to the corn: About a hundred feet from his house was a trail leading up into the woods, where he found ten other ripped-open bags and corn strewed hell, west, and crooked. The bear had been carrying these eighty-pound bags from the garage, leaving no spilled evidence until he got out of sight. As for the bag in the road, the bear had apparently dropped it when the man who reported it came along. Having completed his investigation, my neighbor placed the bag where he could see it under the mercury-vapor light, loaded his rifle, and positioned his chair so that he could keep an eye out for the bear while watching TV. Before long, a pick-up truck came by. It stopped; a man got out, threw the bag in the back, and drove off. Sometimes you just cannot win.

Several local bear hunters then tried to run what we knew must be a very large bear, but to no avail. Next, we put a live-bear trap we'd built in the man's garage. All the bags of the corn the bear so dearly loved were removed, except for about half a bag, which was inside the trap, wired to the trigger. There were also several open-top bags of oats, which we left undisturbed.

In the morning, the trap was unsprung. Missing were two bags of oats. They were not hard to find; two windrows of oats led up the road and into the woods. By the time the bear had arrived with the first bag, the contents were nearly gone. The corn bags had been sewn shut, but not these. Anyway, back he went for another bag, which left another trail.

It was now pretty obvious that we were not dealing with your average bear. The message he left by not going into the trap was clear: He had seen one before. He did not come again after that; the berries got ripe, and that was fine with us. I guess we all hoped some hunter got him that fall.

The following May, we found we hadn't been so lucky. I got a call to come over to see the evidence of the bear's latest visit. This time, he had torn a great gaping hole through a double-planked door on the back side of the potato house. After finding only potatoes, he went across the road and took his usual bag of corn. The bear had to go. I advised Charles Richard, the local game warden, to go ahead and kill the bear. "Great," he said. "Do you have any suggestions?" "It's easy," I said. "Tonight you just get inside one of those grain bags and lay real still." I will not repeat his comment. At quarter of four in the morning, the bear returned. Chuck dropped him from his vantage point in the potato house. The bear was, in fact, a large one, and weighed 333 pounds. So much for that big troublemaker.

Bears, like all other animals (including us humans), are prone to developing habits, many of which tend to fall in the "bad" category. I earlier mentioned the live-bear trap we built; it had seen prior use in a different bear incident—an amusing one, although perhaps not from the bear's viewpoint. The moral of this bear story is that just when you think there can be nothing new, something or other—frequently a bear—will come along with a completely new angle on how to make a nuisance of himself.

Some friends of mine, Rufus Rich and his wife Jane, are the only inhabitants along the twelve-mile road that connects Andover with the South Arm of Richardson Lake. Rufus is well used to living in a remote area, for he lived in the woods when his mother, Louise Dickinson Rich, was writing *We Took to the Woods*, as well as several other books, many years ago. Considering where they live, it was no great surprise when during the summer they began to have a frequent visitor in the form of a bear. What *was* surprising was his boldness.

Fred, as he was promptly named, was no sneak-around-in-the-night–and-rip-open-the-garbage type of bear; he came for his visits in broad daylight. After several visits, he found that the dry dog food on the porch was just to his liking. It quickly became a daily routine to leave some food on the porch for Fred. Each evening before dark, he came and got his supper. With only a screen door separating him from the two family dogs, he would lie with the dish between his paws while he ate; meanwhile, the dogs would lie quietly inside the door and watch him. This was good entertainment, and each evening several cars would pull into the yard to wait for the bear to show up.

Then, after several weeks had passed, the inevitable began to happen. Fred's newly acquired celebrity status began to fade fast, and was replaced with the usual well-earned stigma: that of being a nuisance bear.

We had already been planning to build a trap, and Fred inspired us to get going on it right away. Someone gave me an old fuel drum, and we gathered up some iron and an old boat trailer to mount it on. With the help of some friends who welded and spray-painted the thing, we soon had our trap. Now to catch Fred. I parked the trap near the porch and set it. After wiring the dish of dog food to the trigger inside, I felt confident that, come morning, we would find Fred in the trap.

On my way back the next morning, I stopped at the small store where Jane worked. "No bear," she said. "Did he come back?" I asked. "Oh, sure he did," she laughed. "But he's too smart. He figured out the trap." "What do you mean?" I asked. "Well," she said, "he finally went in the trap, and after he got a mouthful, he came and stood at the back end, looking out while he chewed. He did that a few times, then lay down inside the trap and ate it all, then left. He never moved the dish." The folks in the store thought it was hilarious, and I guess I did, too. "I've got to see this myself," I said. "I'll be up tonight."

That evening, we waited and watched for the bear. Before dark, the dogs suddenly bristled. In a few moments, the bear appeared from the woods. He carefully inspected the trap, then went in. Sure enough, he immediately reappeared at the back and cautiously gazed around while he chewed a mouthful of food. He repeated this several times. "I don't think he understands how the trap is supposed to work," I whispered. Finally, after he apparently decided it was safe enough to be inside, he did not return to the entrance.

Somehow, I knew that this bear of delicate table manners was not going to spring the trap tonight, either. There was only one thing to do, and that was to show him how the door worked. As quietly as possible, I snuck out the Riches' back door and down alongside the camp to the front. At the corner, I peeked around. Fred was still there. Then, covered (I hoped) by the sound of crunching dry dog food as heard by a bear in a steel drum, I crept over to the trap, which was about twenty-five feet away, and yanked the door release. It came down with a tremendous clang; then, all was still.

For about five seconds, it was terribly quiet. Then, poor Fred's manners went all to hell. He hissed and roared and gave the tank some awful swats with his paws. Thank God, it held up. He soon quieted down and behaved. In a few minutes, l drove off, feeling very smug indeed, with Fred rattling along behind. The next morning we escorted him to a place so nice and remote, we knew we wouldn't be seeing him again.

As with humoring moose, sometimes a little Yankee ingenuity is all it takes with bears, as well. Several years ago, a yearling bear took up residence in a large pine tree behind a mobile home. He had apparently come one evening when all was quiet. Then some ducks started a commotion, and he bolted up the nearest tree, which was about four feet from the dwelling. I assured the owner that the bear would come down that night, if he could keep the ducks and any other domestic animals inside the trailer. The next morning, brother bear was still there. I got another call. "Don't worry about it," I told the man. "He'll come down sometime when he gets hungry."

Well, I guess I should not have told him that. The following morning, the bear still had not come down, and was too close for comfort. The man called again. Warden Dave Berry and myself, along with game biologist Phil Bonzenhard, went to the home. By now, there were several spectators, including some children. Phil fired a tranquilizer gun, which, after missing several times, only seemed to drive the bear higher. (I was actually glad Phil did not hit him, for if he had fallen out, the Fish and Wildlife Department would have had to replace one collapsed Sears Roebuck utility shed.)

We stood there and wondered what to do next. Among the spectators was a small boy who came to the fracas armed with a BB gun. "Can I borrow that?" Dave asked. "Sure," said the boy. As fast as he could, Dave began to pelt the bear with BBs from the air rifle. I guess the bear thought he had found a nest of hornets, because he began to jump around in the tree, making a huffing sound. Then, as several more pellets hit him, down he came, and took off like the devil was after him. The kid grinned all over as Dave handed him back the gun and said, "Thank you, young fella."

We occasionally get calls that bears have killed livestock, such as sheep or cattle. Bears are tremendously strong, and can easily kill with one swipe of a paw. I never realized how much power bears have until investigating a complaint that a horse had been killed by one. This was a large workhorse being used in the woods. The owner unharnessed him each night and let him go, and he always went down the road a short way to graze in a clearing at an old camp yard. One morning when the man went after the horse, he found he had been killed by a bear. The horse was dusty and dirty from working, but one could see the spot where he had been struck on the neck. The bear had then eaten some flesh from one of the horse's hindquarters. That evening we made a crude blind downwind, and waited. Before dark, the bear returned, and we killed it. It was a strange-looking bear. He was just skin and bones, but yet weighed 265 pounds. He had been very hungry, maybe even sick.

People, as a rule, seem to be afraid of bears—probably just as well, although most fears are unfounded. From time to time, wardens investigate reports of bears being aggressive, and the problem usually arises from someone blundering unknowingly into a sow-with-cubs situation. This is not always the case, however, and caution and good sense can go a long way in avoiding a "situation" with a bear. The wild ones I trust; it is the semi-wild, no-fear-of-man, live-on-the-dump type of animal that one should be extremely cautious around.

You cannot convince my wife that even the wild bears are safe, and with good reason. Several members of our family were at the family camp on Richardson Lake. Around ten p.m., the power plant was turned off, and everyone turned in. All had been quiet for half an hour or so, when suddenly my wife was poking me in the ribs. Half awake, I mumbled, "What's the matter?" "What's that noise?" she whispered. I did not hear any noise, so I said nothing. She poked me again. "What is that?" she whispered excitedly. Still I heard nothing, but I was at least listening now. We were sleeping on an outside screened porch, and you can always hear noises in the leaves if you listen long enough; a hopping rabbit can sound like a bull moose in dead leaves.

Suddenly, a loud thud shook the camp, and I could hear the definite sound of clapboards being ripped and splintered from the camp. This was no rabbit. We had been broken into by bears before, but never while we were there. In the dark, I found my revolver in my knapsack and hurried out through the living room to the kitchen, where the bear was trying to get in. He was gone, but I heard him crashing through the brush as I fired in the air to keep him going. As you might suspect, the breakfast conversation the next morning ran pretty heavy to bears and our new supply of kindling wood left in a pile beside the camp. That damned bear completely destroyed several years of confidence I had tried to instill in my kids, not to mention my wife, that bears will not bother you if you leave them alone.

By now, you get the picture of what sort of problems bears can create for the warden. A bear can be a most formidable adversary when he so chooses. To wrap up the subject of bears, I must relate this story. Each year, for many years, wardens have attended various sportsmen's shows throughout the country. One year, Sergeant John Robertson, who was a district warden then, was selected to attend the Eastern States Exposition in Springfield, Massachusetts. A warden's function at these shows is to work in the Maine booth and talk to the public and promote the State of Maine. Many states have booths here, and many acquaintances are struck up.

At this particular show, the Vermont booth was located across the aisle from Maine's. During this segment of the show, a sporting camp from Vermont had set up and was promoting bear hunting. Along with large illuminated slides and a mounted bear, they had a cage that held several bear hounds.

At most sportsmen's shows, a special show is usually put on twice a day, once in the afternoon and again at night. During these performances, everything generally stops while folks take in the show; however, one person has to stay and watch over each booth. One of the attractions this year was a man who wrestled a large bear in a ring. All was very quiet in the booths while the show went on.

John, who was manning our booth, happened to look down the aisle and saw the wrestler, complete with leopard-skin Tarzan suit, coming with the bear; the man was leading the bear by a heavy chain. John says, "I was going to say something, but decided I'd just watch." Sure enough, when the bear passed the dog cage, they all lit on the front of it in full cry—upon which the bear bolted by the man and yanked him off his feet. "I leaned forward, and watched him go the whole length of the aisle on his stomach, hanging onto the chain and screaming at the bear. At the end of the aisle, the bear turned right. The man continued straight ahead into another booth, then shot right and disappeared, still hanging onto the chain. I don't know what ever happened after that," says John, "but that was the best damned show I ever saw in my life."

So much for bears.

Deer are usually pretty well behaved. Most of the time, the only problems they create for a warden are directly related to law enforcement. The one disruptive thing they'll frequently do is ravage someone's young apple trees, or maybe make a smorgasbord of someone's garden. Wardens have spent hundreds of hours, in the past, delivering Fish and Wildlife Department–provided repellents to people who are trying to keep deer away.

Each spring it starts all over again. Bone meal (or blood meal, as it is sometimes called) is bought each year by the railroad car, and certain people always want one or two bags of the meal or the strong-scented twine, which we also provide. (These are merely balls of twine dipped in a foul-smelling solution, which deer find offensive enough to keep away from.)

I have always wondered why some people say these things work, and others say they do not. Believe me, a deer or two can certainly raise havoc with the green tops in a garden. I have seen more than one vegetable garden that looked like someone had run it down with a lawn mower. Some folks really get irate, but oddly enough, not many. With apple growers, however, it is a different story. When someone's livelihood is at stake, I guess this is understandable. It takes a lot of fencing to surround a large orchard high enough to keep deer out, and the Fish and Wildlife Department provided this for many years, at considerable expense.

Deer, unfortunately, like blueberries. In Washington County, the blueberry barrens are an important part of the economic picture: Thousands of acres are maintained, and a crop is picked each year. The deer like to help harvest the berries, and years ago this was a very controversial subject. Blueberry field owners had a right to shoot, or hire shot, deer that were doing substantial damage. (Seagulls would flock into these fields by the hundreds, but no one seemed to want to shoot them. Maybe they did not taste as good.) This practice seemed to be anti-conservation, and wardens took a dim view of it. To try to keep a handle on the situation, we asked to be notified when someone had shot a deer so we could check out the crop damage. This could be done, to some extent, by checking the contents of the deer's stomach for berries.

Some people knew it rankled wardens somewhat when these deer were killed. This was evident once when in my absence, an old man contacted my inspector, Gene Mallory, and told him he had killed a deer. Gene told him he would stop by that afternoon. Upon arriving, the man told Gene he was too late; the deer was all cut up. "Well, I'd like to examine the paunch," said Gene. "I buried it," said the man. "Did you cut the paunch open?" asked Gene. "Yes, I did," he said. "Were there any berries in it?" quizzed Gene. "Yes, there were. There were three," said the man, "and one of them was a big one." That is how it goes sometimes.

Anyone who has ever watched Walt Disney, I am sure, has been led to believe that beavers are truly gems of nature. They build amazing dams and houses that are simply works of art. Well, this is right—they accomplish all that, along with a lot of other work that they do not show you. Like many other animals, beavers do well until they and man both try to exist on the same piece of ground.

Wardens and beavers have done battle time and time again. The beaver says, "I guess I'll build my dam here," and the warden says, "Not here, old buddy." I cannot imagine how many thousands of hours wardens have spent over the years, unplugging culverts and bridges to drain the water from flooded roads. Several times each year, most wardens get a complaint from some woodlot owner or farmer whose hayfield is flooded, to do something about those beaver. Digging out beaver dams is so standard a procedure that during much of the year, a potato digger is often a standard piece of equipment in a warden's vehicle. Dynamite is used in areas where it is safe to do so; this is the quickest and surest way to lower the water.

But the culprits who build the dams are extremely persistent and keep rebuilding the dam as fast as it is removed. In some instances, wardens will use a live trap and then relocate the beaver quite a distance away. Many wardens have tried different ways to discourage a beaver from rebuilding his dam. One warden I know placed a dead porcupine at the dam. Next morning, the porcupine was part of the dam. Nothing I know of works for very long. Sometimes, a long box-like device with a hole on the bottom at one end can be placed in the dam. The beaver will often just keep building the dam higher, though he cannot seem to find where the water is leaking from. More often, however, the beaver will have no trouble at all figuring it out.

Once, years ago, a Maine beaver nearly flooded out the Eastern States Exposition. An enclosure was erected for the beaver exhibit. This was quite an elaborate affair, complete with small pond, trees, and bushes. It really was a nice exhibit. The water played over the rocks, and the beaver swam around the pond. Everything was fine until late at night, when the hall was quiet after the show had closed. Everybody knows it is then that a beaver goes about his nightly routine of plugging up the leaks in his dam. The fact that this one was in Springfield, Massachusetts, made no difference to him, so he plugged the drain hole. A frantic phone call to the motel where the Maine crew was staying brought people on the run. Water, water everywhere! On the floor and down through the ceiling to whatever was below, it ran. The beaver from Maine was not welcome anymore.

Despite his general appearance of being a docile animal, a beaver is really nothing to tangle with. I can recall once catching a huge beaver in a live trap. I had to transport him a considerable distance down a railroad track back to my vehicle. I cut a couple of poles, intending to wire one across the trap to lie across the rails, and to use the other one as a draw bar to tow the trap. But there was no way that beaver would let me near the trap. He lunged and hissed and bit each time I tried. It was not until he was worn out that I was able to secure the poles and drag him off.

As I mentioned at the beginning of this chapter, oftentimes the animals we deal with will give us a good laugh. The day-in, day-out episodes all run together after a few years, but the humorous ones always stand out. This one has to be a classic; retired Warden Eben Perry tells the story.

Eben and Warden Martin Savage had gone to the Parmachenee area to blow a beaver dam that was located right beside the road. "It was a sizable dam, but I thought three or four sticks of dynamite would make a good hole," Eben recalls. "Martin thought ten sticks would be better. Well, we were in Martin's district, so ten it was. We buried the dynamite, lit the fuse, and scrambled quickly up over the bank and up the road, as it was a short fuse. After running up the road a ways, we stopped at about the same time that an old blue van appeared. Martin recognized the van as belonging to a Canadian woodcutter, whom, on several prior occasions, he had apprehended for numerous violations, such as illegal partridge and a loaded gun.

"As the vehicle approached, we put our arms up to stop him until the charge went off. He apparently misunderstood our intent, and instead sped up and zoomed past. About the time he passed the dam, it went off, sending a cloud of smoke, mud, water, and sticks into the air with a great bang. We couldn't see him for a few seconds until the smoke cleared. Finally, we caught sight of him way down the road, just rounding a corner on two wheels.

"We left, and this was the end of the story—until sometime later when we stopped at The Brown Owl, a small store just over the state line in Wentworth Location, New Hampshire. The owner asked us what we had done to the man. "Why?" we asked. "Holy cow," he said, "he drove in here like a bat out of hell. When he came in, his eyes were bugged out, and he was all excited, saying, 'By Christ, Hi go back for Canador han never come back here ever, me.' 'What is wrong?' I asked him. 'Hi don no what doze game warden got, but dey was shot at me wit some goddamn big gun!' "

Nearly any animal you can think of can cause a problem if the circumstances are right. Wardens Dwane Duane Lewis and Norman Trask once responded to a call reporting an owl entangled in a chicken-wire fence. As usual, when they arrived, a small group of spectators was present. After considerable effort, they wrapped the owl in a covering and extricated him from the fence. With Norman holding the owl, they drove off. Shortly afterward, the owl managed to get his talons loose, and he embedded them in Norman's abdomen and hung on for dear life. This was no small owl, and it was with great difficulty that he was persuaded to release Norman from his grasp. Maine does not have capital punishment, but I rather think this does not include owls that are latched onto one's stomach. This episode required a trip to the doctor for medical treatment and a tetanus shot.

Fishers are ferocious little animals, and they have an even worse reputation. Warden Francis Cyr was at Ripogenus Dam for many years. Fishers were abundant in his area, so when the Augusta office asked him to trap one live for the game farm, it was no problem. With the fisher in a cage, he and his wife headed for Millinocket. Suddenly, Francis saw that the fisher had gotten out of the cage and was very excited. As fast as he could, he pulled over; the doors flew open, and away went Mr. Fisher. "I decided I didn't need him anymore—at least, not loose in my cruiser," says Francis. I do not know how many folks have ever examined a fisher really closely, but they run pretty heavy to teeth on the front end. They are definitely not something you would want latched onto your ear.

My partner for many years, Elmer Knowlton, and I once nearly had a day's work obliterated by a love-crazed red squirrel. That, I am sure, requires an explanation, so here goes: One evening, on our way home from Sourdnahunk Lake, we swung into a spot where people frequently left their vehicles to go to Slaughter Pond, which is open to fly fishing only. We found a vehicle there, and decided to take the three-and-a-half-mile trail in, to reach the pond shortly after daylight. When we arrived, the party was already on the pond, but they were at the upper end, opposite us. We then cut up into the woods out of sight, and proceeded quickly in their direction. As we reached the other end, we slowed down and made our approach to the shore. Very quietly and slowly we moved, for the canoe was really close to shore.

We had worked our way to within ten yards of shore, when suddenly the stillness was shattered by two red squirrels. We froze in our tracks, knowing the commotion would draw the attention of the people in the canoe our way. One squirrel began chasing the other through the woods, up one tree, then down, and on to the next one. They continued this helter-skelter performance up and down several trees around us for several minutes while we watched. Near where Elmer was standing was a medium-sized dead fir tree, the top half of which had broken off. The broken top was still attached to the upright portion, and the tip touched the ground at his feet. Eventually, the squirrels included this tree in their mad race. Up the tree they went, then down the broken–over top.

When the squirrel being chased reached the bottom, it ran back under the top, out of sight. It was then that the squirrel doing the chasing got to meet Elmer close-up and personal: He reached the ground, ran up Elmer's leg, and stopped right under his chin. There he froze for about ten seconds while they stared at each other, eyeball to eyeball. Elmer's face turned crimson, and his cheeks puffed out like someone blowing up a balloon as he tried to stifle a burst of laughter. From about ten feet away, I was doing the same. I cannot imagine what that squirrel must have thought he had suddenly encountered. Eventually he scampered down and off out of sight, leaving two game wardens half-strangling from wanting to laugh, which we could not do without giving ourselves away. This is what I like about this job: You never know what will happen next—especially if there is an animal involved.

14 — ALWAYS A CHUCKLE

Most game wardens I have encountered over the years have seemed to have a greater appreciation for humorous incidents than people of any other group. I have mentioned this to many of them, and have been offered several reasons as to perhaps why. No one reason seems to completely account for it. One thing I am sure of, though, is that funny incidents occur routinely for us wardens. If nothing should happen incidentally for a while, you can be sure that some-one will soon create a diversion. In fact, it is impossible to get a bunch of wardens together for very long without one pulling a prank on another or someone relating a comical incident.

For a few years after I went to work in the Warden Service, I thought maybe I was the only one with these quirks; then I began to learn that we are nearly all alike. When talking to wardens both working and retired before I began to write this book, I asked many of them why, in their opinion, wardens are so good at get-ting into funny situations, and fond of telling the tales. One retired warden's wife grinned and said she thought it might be a way of relieving the pressures and tensions frequently involved with being a law enforcement officer. I think this may be on the right track. Another factor is that our duties are so diverse at times. This extreme range of activities exposes us to so many different types of situations that a higher-than-ordinary percentage of them fall into the "humorous" category.

When I first went to work, several other young fellows went on at the same time; it was September, with hunting season just around the corner. The following February, we attended the annual Warden School, then a two-week affair at Camp Keyes in Augusta, and those of us who were new would often get together and talk over our first fall as wardens.

The big score of Dick Hennessey's fall was finding a camp in a clearing way back in the woods somewhere in his Monticello district. He had located it in October, and suspected it might be a good place to catch someone Sunday hunting when deer season came. Come November, he got up early one Sunday morning and walked back in to the camp. Sure enough, the camp was occupied. He found a place behind a spruce tree at the edge of the clearing, and began his vigil. By noon, no one had left, other than to make the occasional trip to the outhouse. The afternoon wore on, and it grew colder and windy. It started to snow. His feet began to grow cold, and eventually he was shivering all over, but still he stayed. Finally, around three o'clock, a man walked out on the porch and hollered: "Hey, young fella, why don't you come in and get warm? No one is going hunting from this camp today." He did, and all had a good laugh at his expense. That is the beauty of our cat-and-mouse game—sometimes the laugh is on us. We do not always win, by any means.

I once found a car parked near a bridge at a well-known trout stream. Cautiously, I worked down the stream until I could see the fisherman about fifty yards away. He was squatting down on the bank, fishing a deep hole. I wanted to get very close to him before he saw me, because the brook was loaded with small trout. After making a half-circle away from the brook, I worked very quietly to the spot where he was. Peeking over the bank, I could see him directly under me, still squatting. My approach had had to be a very stealthy one because the stream flowed very quietly and made no rushing noise to cover any twig I might snap. Casually, I stepped up on the bank directly behind him, and stood there about five feet from him. I was going to speak but decided not to, in case he was a jumper. Better to let him see me on his own, I thought. As he fished, he looked up and down the brook but did not look back. Finally, I said, as matter-of-factly as I could, "How are they biting this morning?" He never budged. The guy was stone deaf. I checked his license and left. Now, to be sure, a man who cannot hear is not funny, but I know he would have gotten a chuckle if he had known how long I spent sneaking up on him.

Many people think wardens must have eyes like eagles. There is one man you would have an especially hard time convincing otherwise. Warden Duane Lewis once checked a fisherman on Grand Lake Stream. After chatting with him awhile, Duane asked him if he was alone. "Oh, no," he replied. "My buddy is downstream, somewhere around the corner." "What is his name?" asked Duane. "Stanley Wasaloski," said the man. "Where's he from?" quizzed Duane. "Sanford," replied the fisherman. "Thanks a lot," said Duane. Downstream a ways, Duane found the man wearing chest waders, fishing far out in a pool some distance from shore. The man noticed Duane standing on shore and hollered, "I suppose you want to see my license, don't you?" "Yes," hollered Duane, "but you don't have to come all the way over here. Just hold it up so I can see it." With a somewhat puzzled look, the man fumbled for his wallet inside his waders. He opened it and held up his license. Duane squinted and shaded his eyes with one hand. "Stanley Wasaloski, Sanford, Maine. Okay, thanks a lot," he hollered, then left. The man looked at his license, shook his head, and put it back in his wallet.

We all know how our best-laid plans can sometimes go afoul. Wardens are in no way immune from this phenomenon. Merrymeeting Bay is, by far, Maine's best-known duck-hunting area. Each fall, hunters arrive here in numbers that at times appear to exceed the ducks. The potential here is tremendous for violations ranging from early shooting, taking over the limit, and late shooting. Therefore, teams of wardens traditionally are called in to hopefully keep violations to a minimum.

On one occasion, the day's hunt had drawn to a close. Hunters had gathered their tollers and, as near as wardens could tell, there were only two parties left. It got later and later, and still the parties stayed. The wardens watched them, expecting that one or the other group would shoot late. It eventually got too dark to shoot, so everyone left, including the wardens. When the wardens beached their boat at the Bowdoinham camp, all three groups met, and discovered that three groups of wardens had all been watching one another. It sure was nice when we all got walkie-talkies.

More often than not, though, it is the simplest, most spontaneous incidents that get us laughing the hardest. Many years ago, Warden Basil Closson walked into a backwoods trout pond. He had carried in a small canoe. Upon arriving, he saw a canoe on the pond with three occupants, two of whom were fishing. The third was asleep in the bottom of the canoe. As Basil prepared to paddle out, one of the men hollered to him. "We've been driving all night and would like to have breakfast. Is it permissible to build a fire on shore?" "It's okay by me," Basil answered. "Come on over." At this point, the man asleep in the canoe stood up and stretched; then, apparently in his half-awake stupor, he assumed they had landed and stepped over the side into the pond, which was quite deep at that spot. His companions, in their hilarity, nearly upset the canoe while fishing him out. They finally made shore, and all four men had another great laugh. Don't you wish you could get to see something like that, just once?

Maine humor is noted for being rather dry, as you know. The closer to the coast you go, the drier it seems to get; it must be the salt air. Several years ago, a law was passed that made it illegal to use an artificial light to illuminate wild birds or game after a certain date in the fall. An old man in Leonard Ritchie's Lubec district had raised a large garden, which he had harvested. Included in the garden was a turnip patch, which he had left, as one does with turnips. Several deer had discovered the tops, which they love, and were coming nightly to feed on them. The garden was in a remote area, and the deer were fairly vulnerable to night hunters. Leonard spent many hours that fall watching the turnip patch and apprehended several violators, which pleased the old man immensely, as he liked having the deer around. One day late into the fall, Leonard met the old fellow in the local store. "Say, young fella," he said, "you must be 'bout done with my turnips. Okay if I take 'em up?"

In another incident, a local old-timer complained to Leonard that a bear had gotten into his beehives. "Why don't you set a bear trap?" Leonard asked. "I ain't got one," he replied, "but by Gawd, I know where there is one. That's what I'll do." A day or two later, Leonard saw him and asked how he had made out with the bear trap. "Not very well," he answered. "I set it that night. When I went up in the mornin', there was a rabbit in it. Sitting right on the pan, he was. Gawd, warn't he caught some solid."

Sometimes, Maine humor defies logic unless you live here. Once, after a snowstorm, I observed an elderly gentleman I knew who had gotten his car slightly off over the edge of his driveway and was shoveling it out. I stopped and walked over. "What's the matter?" I said. "You stuck?" He never looked up. Finally he stopped. He studied his predicament a moment, wiped his nose with his mitten, then said, "Waal, I guess I would be if I was goin' someplace."

Retired chief warden Alanson "Mickey" Noble once had a friend who had a fox farm years ago. One day a car stopped, and two ladies walked over to the pen to admire the foxes. The man who owned the farm walked over. "Oh, what beautiful animals," one lady remarked. "Ayuh, they ain't too bad," said the man. "Tell me something," she said, "How often do you pelt those foxes?" Definitely amused, but not wanting to embarrass her in front of her friend, he replied, "Oh, 'bout once a year, as a rule. Makes 'em goddamned nervous, too."

Usually several times in a warden's career, someone will not recognize him when he is out of uniform—and sometimes even when he is wearing it. The results can be hilarious. Several wardens and myself were attending a trappers' field day in Bethel one time. There were at least two hundred people milling about. Several wardens, a rather devious Baxter State Park ranger named Tom Chase, Monty Washburn, and myself were standing in a group. As we talked, I saw a man I knew coming my way. I could not place him or put a name on him, but recognized him as someone I had known for some reason somewhere. He stuck out his hand, and we all shook it.

"I'm glad to see you fellows turn out," he said. "I think it's great. I don't seem to know any of you fellows, but I do know a couple of game wardens." "Really," I asked. "Who are they?" "Well," he said, "I know Rod Sirois." "Yes," I said, "I know Rod." "I know Eric Wight," he said. "You know Eric? Hell, I know him, too," I replied. "Do you?" he asked. "Oh sure," I said. I shot a glance at Monty, who was now looking up in the sky. My friend Chase then offered, "I heard he's a mean sonuvabitch."

"Oh, well, he's not too bad," says the man. "He pinched me once years ago for over the limit of smelts. It was my own fault, though. He's okay." At this point I crossed my arms to cover my name tag and shot another glance at Washburn, hoping for some help. No help from him. He had his back turned now, his shoulders moving up and down in silent laughter and wiping his eyes with his handkerchief. As quick as he had come, the man said, "See you later, boys, gotta go." "Bye—it's been fun talking with you," I answered.

Things of this nature happen off and on, but in terms of humor would be called soft-core, I suspect. The rough stuff seems to happen between the wardens themselves. This is where the tension I spoke of is let off. One obviously cannot play very rough on the general public, so the fun is made amongst ourselves.

Fall and the long nights can sometimes be brightened up and made more tolerable with a little fun. Anyone who is prone to going to sleep can usually expect something unusual to happen to him before long. If he is lucky, it might be something mild, like having the batteries in his flashlight replaced by sand. I know of one warden who had this done to him and discovered the apparent case of dead batteries when he got home. He proceeded to dump them on the bed so as to replace them with fresh ones, but reportedly his wife did not appreciate the charge of sand dumped on her bed, especially since she was already in it.

The story goes that this same warden was asleep in the back of another warden's car one night when they pulled in to drop him off at home. The warden driving the car lurched to a sudden stop. Flinging the doors open, the two wardens in front hollered, "There they are. Get 'em!" Instantly up but not fully awake, the backseat warden rushed over and yanked the door open on his own car. Nice guys.

Believe me when I say nothing is sacred, not even a man's bird hunting. Two wardens are going along an old road. The wardens Dave Berry and Ted White are best of friends. It is bird season, and a bird is spotted. Dave stops. "Here, try these shells, Ted." A careful aim, then Ted fires. A great white cloud of flour appears, which slowly blows back in Ted's face. "Did you get him, Ted? Huh? Did you get him?" Berry is convulsed in the truck. Ted mumbles something about Dave's questionable ancestry and climbs back in. Some people just are not safe to be around. This same guy once snuck into someone's office and glued down the receiver on a desk phone with super glue, then had someone call, just to watch.

Some of the older wardens have told me about pranks that happened years ago. If anything, wardens were even worse then than we are now. Several wardens were staying in the old Naples warden camp during the smelt run. Per usual, you stumbled into camp wet and cold in the early hours of the morning, wanting only to get in your sleeping bag, get warm, and go to sleep. As frequently happens in any group of men, no matter who they are, one does not fit. On this occasion, it was a warden who, in Raymond Curtis's words, had to "fart around for half an hour, washing his face, brushing his teeth, shaving, and putting his pajamas on before turning out the light and being still."

Several steps were taken to ensure this man knew how much he was appreciated. These measures included putting a baby porcupine in his sleeping bag, oleomargarine in the crotch of his pajamas, and fox scent in his aftershave lotion. One by one he discovered these, and without a word, packed his wanigan to leave. He left in such a huff that when his car fetched up on the thirty-foot hawser rope tied to his bumper, I guess he damn near broke his neck. It goes without saying that he never came down to work the smelt run again.

Warden camps have always been a great spot for this type of fun. Another story involved several wardens spending the night in the Albany camp years ago. One warden wore false teeth. Upon retiring each night, he placed his teeth in a glass of water. After he had gone to sleep, another warden, who had been an undertaker's assistant prior to becoming a warden, replaced them with another set he had been saving for just such an occasion. The following morning, when the warden arose, he grabbed his teeth, popped them in his mouth, and stepped outside to relieve himself. As he stood there doing so, he gnashed on the teeth. He took them out several times, examined them, and put them back in—to no avail. "Well, Goddammit, they always did fit," he cursed. The camp erupted in laughter. "Here, try these," someone hollered. Knowing he'd been had, he stormed back inside. No, sir, this is no place for someone who cannot take a joke.

Humor—like beauty, I suppose—is in the eye of the beholder: It is always funnier if it happens to someone else. However, on this job, at least, it is essential to be able to laugh at yourself from time to time. And, sooner or later, it will be your turn.

Some stories take on an almost legendary status. One of those that comes to mind involved some wardens who were watching a camp full of Canadians one night whom they suspected were night hunting in the choppings nearby. One of the wardens present spoke French, so it was suggested that he get close to the camp to listen; it would be helpful to know if the conversation inside the camp included any mention of night hunting.

He crept alongside the camp. Through a window he could observe and listen quite well. At some point, a man suddenly slid his chair back from the table and started for the door. Not wishing to be discovered, the warden quickly knelt down and crawled under the camp. In doing so, he made a noise as he crawled over some old boards. The fellows in the camp heard this, and he heard them decide it must be a porcupine. Someone quickly grabbed the teakettle from the stove and began pouring hot water through the cracks in the floor above where they thought the varmint was to drive him away. It worked, so they say.

Occasionally, you don't get to be in on the actual culmination of some prank or incident, and can only chuckle and wonder at the final outcome. Once, my fellow warden Elmer Knowlton and I were attempting to take a shortcut over a rough road that eventually led to the good road we wanted. After bouncing over rocks and ruts for about two miles, we had come within two hundred yards from the good road. At this point, we came to a pup tent pitched squarely in the middle of the road. There was no room to go around. No one seemed to be there, but camping gear was left in and around the tent.

Elmer and I both had the same idea. After pulling all the poles and removing the bags and mattresses, we moved the pots and pans aside, laid the tent down flat, and drove over it. Then we carefully put the tent poles back, put everything back inside, replaced the pots and pans, and continued on. Everything was exactly as they had left it, with the exception of two dusty tire tracks across the tent. "Bet they won't sleep so good tonight," Elmer chuckled.

When someone is apprehended at committing a violation, the only thing to do often seems to be to make the best of a bad situation. A little humor is relished by everyone, especially when the jig is up. We once confronted a subject in a boat on Sourdnahunk Lake, having watched him plenty long enough to know he was not fly-fishing, as is the law there. He insisted, however, that he was fly-fishing, so Elmer asked him to reel in his line. He did so, and as the fly cleared the water, a long, so-called "Garden Hackle" was dangling from his fly. "My God, look at that," he exclaimed. "I've caught a worm." "No kidding," Elmer said. "How do you suppose it got on there?" "I don't know," the man said. "He was right here in my pocket just a few minutes ago."

One might ordinarily assume that within the halls of our judicial system, there is not much room for humor. This, however, is far from true. Some real gems occur in these places. Wardens and attorneys meet in court along with the judge, day in and day out, attempting to resolve someone's predicament according to the guidelines of our judicial system. In many cases, the matter is settled by plea-bargaining between the attorneys and never reaches the courtroom. No matter how sincere our attempts at maintaining the impression of the seriousness of the matter at hand, sooner or later, something amusing is bound to happen.

On one occasion, a warden was on the stand giving testimony in a night hunting case. He had testified that the vehicle in question had stopped and a light had been shone into a field. "How long would you say the light was visible?" asked the defense attorney. "About a minute," the warden replied. "Couldn't it have been half a minute?" asked the attorney. "No, it was a minute," replied the warden. "How do you know it was a minute?" queried the attorney. "I just do," said the warden.

"This is amazing," said the attorney. "With the court's permission, I'd like to have the warden demonstrate his amazing ability to estimate time so precisely." The judge nodded. "When I say go," said the attorney, "I'd like you to tell me when you think a minute has passed. Go!" said the attorney as he looked at his watch. "Now," said the warden. The attorney shook his head. "You're right," he exclaimed. "One minute exactly."

There were no more questions along that line, and the case continued. Eventually the subjects were convicted of night hunting. After the trial, the attorney approached the warden in the hall. "Well, you got me on that one," he remarked. "I'm curious, though; how the hell do you do that? Do you count to yourself, or what?" With a grin, the warden led him down the hall to the courtroom door. "See that?" he said as he pointed to a large clock with a sweep second hand hung on the back wall of the room.

Night hunting is one of the most serious violations that wardens try to combat. Over the years, undercover wardens have briefly infiltrated the ranks of night hunters while posing as out-of-state hunters. From time to time, they are able to buy a deer from someone. When they are successful, they give the information to the local warden, then leave without revealing their identity. The warden then issues the summons to the party involved in the illegal sale. Sometimes the respondent simply pleads guilty and pays the fine. Occasionally, though, someone will hire a lawyer and want a trial.

In one such case, the three undercover wardens came to Houlton Court on the trial date in uniform. The defendant sat in the courtroom, waiting for the trial to begin. At some point, his attorney walked through the hall and noticed the wardens. Since he had not ever seen them, he stepped to the courtroom door and motioned for his client to come out. "Have you ever seen these men before?" he asked him. His client looked at them a second, then blurted, "Jesus Christ! Those are the guys I sold the deer to." There was no trial. He was quickly advised to withdraw his plea and pay the fine.

Even judges are not completely above courtroom humor. Although they do not indulge in it, sometimes the situation at hand is just plain humorous and cannot be denied. Warden Carroll Bates and myself once had two subjects before the bench in Houlton on an illegal-possession–of-deer-meat charge. The judge was from Bangor and had the reputation of being one of the sterner judges. He tolerated no haphazard proceedings, and we were on our toes. One subject pleaded guilty and was assessed a fine considerably higher than normal.

The second subject was then called. As he stood before the bench while the charge was read, I think he decided he should at least say something in his own behalf. When the judge was through, the man offered this explanation. "Your Honor," he began, "I've been drunk for several days. I don't really know what's been going on. This meat was apparently brought into my house—by whom, I do not know." The judge pondered this briefly. Then, looking down over his glasses and in a very serious tone, he suggested, "Some phantom, perhaps?"

One evening just prior to dark many years ago, I had retrieved a pheasant from the trunk of a fellow's car and summonsed him to Calais Court for possession of the pheasant in closed season. A day or two previously, we had released a number of pheasants in this area. Unfortunately, this particular man, who spent his days working in a large truck garden nearby, had yielded to the temptation and shot one. The judge asked him why he had done this. He explained to the judge that during that morning, as he worked, he had from time to time noticed this object down at the end of one of the rows.

"What was this object you speak of?" asked the judge. "Well, to be perfectly honest, I didn't know what it was, Your Honor," he replied. "What did you think it might be?" said the judge. "I thought it might be a porcupine," he answered. "Really?" said the judge. "Yep," the man replied. "Tell me, have you had trouble with porcupines eating your garden?" quizzed the judge. "Nope, not yet," he said. "So you shot it," said the judge. "Yep, that's right, I did," he answered. "Well, after you shot it, did you know what it was then?" asked the judge. "Nope, I thought I'd take it home and ask somebody," he replied. "Look," said the judge, "have you ever worn glasses?" "Nope," came the reply. "Well listen," said the judge, "I strongly recommend that you make an appointment as soon as possible with a competent optometrist, because I sincerely believe you must need glasses. The court finds you guilty, and that will be fifty dollars."

Sometimes it is very difficult to keep a straight face until you get outside.

As you have already gathered, courtroom humor is frequently at someone else's expense. This next incident got a lot of chuckles from everyone except the attorneys.

One winter day, I had been patrolling in a plane with Warden Pilot Dick Varney. Upon our return landing, we taxied over to my vehicle. As we drew near, I observed some sort of a lump under the cover of my snowmobile. "Don't leave yet," I advised him. "Lord knows what it is." I loosened the cover and reached underneath, grabbed whatever it was, and yanked it out. Well, I would have guessed it was quite a lot of things before I would have arrived at an artificial leg, complete with harness.

It was a beauty, flesh-colored and all. Dick shook his head and took off, leaving me to admire my new acquisition. At this point, the joke was on me; I even had someone in mind as the per-petrator. But, if you do not wear one, there is not much you can do with something like this; I doubt if it would even sell at a yard sale.

There had to be some use for it, however. The following Monday morning, I took it to court. Arriving early, I took it into the room where the officers and attorneys congregated each morning prior to court. Several officers showed up, and we all chuckled over my good fortune. After a while, a lawyer arrived and, following some chitchat, got his eye on the prosthesis, which was stood upright in the corner. "What the hell is that doing here?" he exclaimed. "Well, I'll tell you," I said. "I've been coming to court for many years, and time and time again I've seen you lawyers in here with some client who didn't have a leg to stand on. So, here's one for anyone who might need one." Decency will not allow me to repeat his comment. You do not get many chances like that.

From time to time, as I mentioned, it comes your turn, and you had best grin and take it. It's hard sometimes. Sometimes it's a lot harder than others.

Jim Welch and I once put his boat into Rangeley Lake to work. Just as we got ready to shove off, I remembered my binocu-lars. I ran over to my vehicle, unlocked the door, and leaned across the seat to grab them. At this instant, a hornet with a stinger that must have looked like a twenty-penny spike nailed me right where one's body normally comes in contact with a boat seat. My reaction was sudden enough to hit my head on the roof of the car, and now I had a sore head, besides. Luckily, the boat had high sides; otherwise, Jim would have rolled out in his fit of laughter. Of course, when we got out on the lake, there was a considerable breeze, which did not add much for the person in the bow. Have you ever tried to ride in a bow of a boat on a windy day supporting yourself with your hands? It may be funny, but it's not all that much fun.

To conclude this chapter, I would like to relate an incident that I think may best illustrate just what can happen to provide a little humor on what might have been an ordinary night in the lives of two game wardens.

Warden Lloyd Davis, who had the Medway area years ago, was on foot with another warden one night. With their sleeping bags under their arms, they were on their way to watch some back fields that they had reason to suspect were being night-hunted from time to time. After crossing several fields, they came to one they knew a bull was pastured in. In the dark, they stopped at the fence to listen and look for the bull. To not cross this field meant added distance. Convinced that the bull was in another part of the pasture, they went over the fence and started across.

"We got about halfway across," Lloyd recalls, "when we heard him coming. We ran like hell for the only tree in the field, which was a large skunk spruce, dropped our sleeping bags, and went up as high as we could. The bull snorted and pawed the ground, and we wished the tree was higher. He then discovered the sleeping bags on the ground. Mine was an old, ratty thing that had come out of a warden camp somewhere; the other fellow had a brand-new one he had hardly even used. Well, the bull pawed that new bag all to shreds, and never even looked at mine. Finally, the bull wandered off. Each time we thought he might be gone, we tried to get down. Then he'd hear the limbs cracking, and come charging back. That cussed bull kept us up there till darn near day-light. That was a long, cold night, let me tell you!"

15 — SEASON TO SEASON

Most people would agree, I think, that it is quite natural for the parents of any youngster to hope that he might someday become successful, even to the point where he would be considered outstanding in some particular field. This has certainly come true in the case of my parents. Since becoming a game warden twenty-odd years ago, I have stood out in more fields than you can imagine. These would include hay fields, clover fields, and occasionally even blueberry fields. I wonder sometimes if that is exactly what they had in mind. It is only in fun I mention this, of course, but it seems like a good way to lead into this chapter about a warden's work.

When you hear people discussing this game warden or that one, you are apt to hear things like, "He's a sneaky sonuvabitch," or "He'd pinch his own grandmother." Well, you get used to that in time, but nevertheless, this is apparently the stigma often associated with game wardens. There is no denying that when a warden is attempting to apprehend fish and game law violators, he often has to be very clever at concealing himself in order to be effective. You had better believe that most poachers also fall into this category, and are always scheming up ways to outwit the game warden. I once was talking to a fellow warden who was planning to retire in the near future. I said, "How come you want to retire, anyway?" He shook his head and said, "You know . . . twenty years is a long time to hide behind a tree." What he said was absolutely true. As a warden gets older, the nights he spends out seem to get longer and longer, not to mention colder.

There is no doubt that a game warden does prowl around in the woods both day and night. It is a very important aspect of his job. It is understandable, then, that people frequently view him in this regard. There are, however, many more aspects to his job than most people realize. Many of the things I have written about here have been exciting or perhaps humorous incidents. These are easy to write about, for they stand out as highlights. In actuality, a warden's job has its high points and its low points, just like any other occupation.

So that the reader will not get the impression that a warden's life is all just one adventure after another, I will relate some of the basic "nuts and bolts" aspects of being a game warden.

The Maine Warden Service in itself is outstanding in many ways. One of these is that, as far as I am able to learn, it is the oldest organized agency of its type in America. Since the days long ago, when a warden received a badge and a law book upon being hired, things have progressed to the point where Maine game wardens have long been recognized for being as well equipped as wardens anywhere. The equipment issued to each man now includes uniforms, several types of boots, a radio-equipped pickup truck, a portable radio, a boat and motor, a canoe, a snowmobile, and (lately) three-wheeled ATVs (all-terrain vehicles). This at first may seem like a great variety of vehicles, but when you consider that Maine is somewhat over 300 miles long and 200 miles wide, with several distinct differences in terrain, this variety of equipment makes somewhat more sense, and in fact is absolutely essential if a mere 100 game wardens are expected to enforce the fish and game laws to any appreciable extent throughout the 33,000 square miles of Maine.

Maine's great variety of weather (for which we are famous), along with these differences in terrain, all contribute to the diversity of the situations encountered by wardens. This is illustrated by the fact that wardens in southern Maine may have been checking boaters and fishermen for several weeks in the spring, while their northern counterparts are still riding snowmobiles or checking deer yards on snowshoes.

Believe me, it is extremely interesting to have a job that is done nearly 100 percent in the out-of-doors, both in daylight and darkness, good weather and bad, that changes with each season. How many other occupations are there where one might find oneself helping to airlift some caribou onto Mount Katahdin one day and helping to stock fish the next? (The caribou airlift, by the way, was an experiment made by the Fish and Game Department in the early 1960s to see if these animals could be reestablished in Maine. Several were trapped, then trucked from Newfoundland to Baxter State Park. They were then lifted by helicopter to the Tableland, where, years ago, caribou wintered on the windswept plateau. The following spring, as the snows melted, they dropped down off the mountain. Several sightings were reported to wardens and biologists for two or three years. Then they disappeared completely.)

Starting in January, wardens have a great many activities to keep them busy. The ice fishermen and beaver trappers are out in force, along with rabbit hunters. A warden spends many hours of his time during the winter months on snowmobile and snowshoes, checking for possible violations pertaining to these activities. During this time, deer yards are also of prime concern, and he is expected to keep track of activities in these areas. He makes frequent checks on them, watching for evidence of poaching or predation by coyotes and domestic dogs. Snow depth is a prime factor in rating the severity of winter, and is also a prime factor in the survivability of deer. A warden frequently assists the game biologists in their efforts by checking snow depths and gathering information on any dead deer he finds.

In his wintertime travels, the warden will inspect any private camps he runs across. Quite frequently, someone has left a door open or a camp may possibly have been broken into. Most camp owners appreciate this service greatly. In a deep-snow winter, the great weight can cause a camp to go down. More than a few people have received a phone call from the local warden with the bad news of such an occurrence.

As winter wears along into March and the snow becomes crusty, the warden will receive complaints of dogs chasing deer. This problem has existed for many years, although it has been tremendously reduced by virtue of the statewide leash law. For many years, it was so bad in central and southern Maine that wardens from northern Maine spent several weeks each spring helping wardens in these areas to control the problem. It was common for several hundred deer each spring to die due to being chased by domestic dogs. In recent years, as coyotes have become more numerous, they, too, have taken a great many deer in some areas. It frequently seems that deer do not have much going for them. Each and every year, many deer, as well as moose, are struck by vehicles. Wardens respond to these incidents and make out an accident form on each one.

With the arrival of spring, the snowmobiles are put away, and out come the boats and canoes. Canoeing has become very popular in Maine in recent years. Unfortunately, many folks do not understand that the high, ice-cold water is extremely dangerous if there should be a mishap. Each spring, wardens and divers have the grim task of searching for drowned victims. In April, hundreds of boaters and fishermen take to the water as fast as it becomes ice-free. For weeks, the warden is extremely busy, checking open-water fishermen by day and working the hundreds of smelt brooks, both closed and open, by night. Going day and night during this time, he always sighs with great relief when the smelts are finally done running.

May quickly becomes June, bringing new activities. People's gardens start to sprout everywhere, and the deer quickly discover them. When the warden gets home for supper, he frequently finds that several people have called during the day and want to obtain some of the various repellents available from Fish and Wildlife.

In an average summer, a warden will spend many hours on the water, enforcing the boating regulations. If he has what we call a woods district, he will undoubtedly spend many hours on foot, checking brooks or watching for illegal activities on the dozens of small, remote ponds that have special regulations. Wardens in these areas will also spend a considerable amount of time each summer looking for someone who is overdue, or trying to locate someone on vacation in order to deliver an important message. These attempts to locate a person can sometimes be very frustrating. More often than not, someone from out of state calls and wants so-and-so to call home immediately on a matter of utmost urgency—injury, sickness, even death. All too frequently, however, the warden is only given the name of a party who may be camped in the Moosehead area, or perhaps on a St. John River trip. Sometimes it is pretty difficult to find these people, but we always try.

With July comes what is, to some people, the beginning of

deer season. Complaints of night hunting come in from time to time, pleasing the warden no end. If sitting out nights in the fall is not bad enough, try sitting out in the summer, killing no-see-ums, blackflies, and mosquitoes! At least there are no flies in November. Before busy fall comes, each warden is obliged to attend a week-long in-service training program each summer at the Maine Criminal Justice Academy in Waterville. Here, he receives updated training in such areas as first aid and search and seizure laws. During this week, he must also successfully qualify with his service revolver, as required by Maine law. He is expected to participate in a physical training program, which includes a one-and-a-half-mile run. (This particular segment proved one thing to me: Prior to the run, I had no idea my tongue was that long. Much of a game warden's work is of a physical nature, and from time to time requires a fair amount of endurance.)

As summer winds down, everything else begins to pick up. The leaves begin to turn, and the nights have a chill to them. The warden now spends many more nights out on patrol. Bear hunters begin to arrive at the many bear-hunting lodges in northern Maine. It is still fishing season until the end of September, and a warden has to divide his time accordingly. From then into October, a warden may spend some time assisting hatchery men in stocking fish in the lakes and ponds within his district. Warden pilots spend many hours stocking fish by plane in dozens of remote, inaccessible ponds. Also, for a great many years, pheasants were raised and released by the hundreds by wardens each fall throughout Maine.

When October finally arrives, things are just slightly less hectic for a game warden than in November. Trappers are now afield, along with raccoon hunters, bear hunters, duck hunters, rabbit hunters, and partridge and woodcock hunters. It is very seldom during October that a warden ever gets to do half the things he had hoped to do on any one given day. You may have hoped to get up early and canoe down some marsh, checking muskrat trappers. A car-deer collision at four a.m. assured that you got up early—and that is as far as you got. Someone calls and has found an illegally shot moose. You spend all day investigating and taking care of the moose. The two hindquarters are gone, and the rest is spoiled. Someone then calls and reports that something has killed some sheep. Off you go to investigate that. That evening, you go out on patrol with a fellow warden. Plans are made to work the marsh again tomorrow. Before you can get away in the morning, however, some trapper calls you to say that someone has stolen some of his traps and he knows who it is—will you come over right away? Oh well, maybe you'll get to the marsh tomorrow.

Wardens in the northern part of Maine are involved to a great extent each fall with the annual weeklong moose hunt. During the first three years in which the hunt was conducted, a gun holiday was declared, banning all other hunting during that week. In 1984, no holiday was invoked. This created a few more problems, but all in all, it went well. Wardens from different parts of Maine are assigned to northern areas for the duration of the hunt to help ensure that things go smoothly. I have been fortunate enough to return each year to the area where I once worked. I must say that after working so many years protecting moose with no open season at all, it still gives me a start to come around a corner and see someone loading one, all perfectly legal. I guess it is just hard to undo something that has been ingrained in one's thinking for so long.

Once the moose hunt is over, the final countdown to deer season begins. From a warden's point of view, I doubt that there is any way to describe a Maine deer season. It might be described as one long blur of activity, with tiny periods of naps and rests in between. The activities a warden is involved in during this time are simply too numerous to mention. They range from lost hunters to night hunters to—unfortunately—the occasional hunting accident. Game wardens are mandated by the attorney general's office in Maine to conduct these investigations and to prosecute, when possible, under criminal law. A considerable amount of training is involved in the proper procedures for the preparation of such cases. More fortunate is the fact that in later years, the number of these incidents has been greatly reduced by fluorescent orange and hunter safety courses. By the time the hunt is over, you can be sure that Maine game wardens have earned a rest.

Somewhere around the time I went to work, I recall being given a book that told in great depth about the duties of a game warden. About the only thing I really remember is that in the very beginning, it said a game warden had to wear many hats. Whoever wrote that knew what he was talking about. One evening a warden may find himself a guest speaker at some function until nine p.m. or so. Two hours later, he may be dressing off a road-killed moose in the pouring rain, or miles from his truck, tracking a lost hunter. The next day, he might be watching someone's traps, hoping to catch whoever has been stealing the trapper's fur. It goes on in this manner, day in and day out, season after season, year after year. It gets in a person's blood, somehow, and there seems to be no way to turn it off. There are few dull moments in a game warden's career. About the time you think things have calmed down a mite, something invariably happens, and you are off again. Actually, I think most wardens thrive on this, and would not wish it any other way. I know I wouldn't.

16 — So You Want to Be a Game Warden

Let me tell you about the first time I heard those words. It was in early October, 1963. I had been a warden for about two weeks, and was living in the warden camp in Township 18 in Washington County. It was about one a.m. A light rain was falling, and it was darker than hell. Inspector Gene Mallery, Warden Leonard Ritchie, and myself had left our vehicle and walked some distance, and were now hunkered down under some fir trees at the edge of a field. It was very damp, and the only sounds were those of an occasional car passing some distance away and of large drops of water dripping from the limbs and spatting on the wet leaves around us. My thoughts were a couple of hundred miles away with my wife and our three-week-old son, whom I hoped to bring as soon as I could find a place to live. It was when the dampness began to soak through and we became a bit uncomfortable that Gene spoke: "So you want to be a game warden." It was not a question, just a statement. Now, twenty-two years later, I would have to say, "Yes, I guess I do."

I think it would be interesting to look at what it means to be a warden, from not only my perspective, but from others', as well. We will take a look at what is involved in a game warden's make-up and things he believes in. I can truthfully say that I know of no occupation that puts a person to a greater variety of tasks, all lumped under one title. It is this wild variety that keeps us going year in, year out. As the seasons change, so does a warden's work schedule and his associated priorities. But, more than that, what seemingly indescribable force is there that compels a person to want this type of life? Well, that is a good question. After many years, I am not sure I know, but I do have some thoughts. (I have often had the same thoughts about someone who becomes a monk in a monastery.)

Let us suppose that you have decided to become a warden. Now, after you have taken all the tests and passed them, you are sworn in and are now a member of the Maine Warden Service. What will you need to be successful? You have your equipment from the storehouse; I am referring to those things that are not issued—qualities, many of which you will need to develop. If you have passed the preliminary tests, it is pretty well established that you possess the basics, such as honesty and integrity, so what is left?

Well, there is patience, for starters. Maybe you thought patience was what you had while waiting for fish to bite. This is true, but you will have to learn to have a great deal more. Aside from honesty, patience is perhaps the most important virtue you need to be a game warden. You must learn to sit for hours on end, night after night, in some dark field or closed smelt brook. Maybe it means sitting all day, watching some fly-fishing-only pond while you kill blackflies. This may take a while to learn; and for the first years of your career, you will waste many miles and hours trying to be everywhere in your whole district at least once a day, because someone may be doing something they should not. As you go on, you will discover, as your patience increases, that you can produce more work with less effort.

Another requirement of the job (which you will hopefully learn in time) is to become extremely observant. You may already be very observant when you start out, and if so, this is to your advantage. Learning to take notice is where an older, experienced warden can teach you much; no books can help you here. What will you learn? For one thing, you will learn never to overlook anything you see, no matter how insignificant it may seem. Tracks in snow are very apparent; they are not so apparent on bare ground, especially if someone has taken means to conceal his comings and goings. You will learn to observe animals and their various habits, which affect poachers and their habits, which in turn affect your own work efforts. You will learn to observe how poachers operate, and be able to tuck this knowledge away in your mind for future reference, when your instant recall will be to your advantage, not his. Your ability to observe will substantially increase your effectiveness as a warden.

I recall once, in September, stopping to examine a slight scuff mark in a remote gravel road. This turned out to be where a deer had been shot a day or so earlier. A small amount of blood and hair was found in the bushes where the deer had lain. We found a spent .22 shell up the road a few feet, and before the afternoon was over, had gone to a house twenty miles away, gotten the meat, and issued a summons for illegal possession of deer meat. There was a lot of luck involved, granted, but the point is, it all started with a small mark in the road. Never overlook or assume anything, if you are a game warden.

The third thing you will need to acquire as a warden is a good deal of dignity. Remember, no one likes a sore loser. It is one thing to walk off the field with your head up after losing a high school football game. It is quite another matter to have four subjects found not guilty of illegally possessing a deer killed in the nighttime, especially when you caught them with it. When the judge orders you to return the deer, and they drive up to your car in the parking lot, grab the deer, and drive off laughing, you had best have a firm grip on your dignity. That is why the coach always said, If you did your best, do not hang your head. Remember that in one moment you can lose your dignity, and see it suddenly reappear as a tarnished spot on the high degree of professionalism you must strive to maintain. No one wins all the time.

Perseverance. Remember, you are probably going to be a warden for many years. In this job, you probably won't reap any great rewards or see any substantial reduction in the number of violators from year to year. In fact, it may well increase. Warden Bruce Farrar explains it this way: "It's not like a woodpile you worked on all day, and when you're through can say, 'There!' and stand back to admire it. The results are not of a tangible nature. It is something you have to believe in very deeply, hoping that your contribution is one worthwhile to the overall long-term conservation effort."

He is right, I think. If you do not learn to persevere, you may find yourself in a rut after a few years. The rut can then become a trench so deep, no one even knows you are in there. Believe this, I have seen it happen. If you are a new warden, you probably have no reason to think about perseverance. Somewhere down the road, however, you will understand what it takes to maintain the drive to continue to go check that same pond several times a week during the summer and apprehend no one. Maybe it is seldom that you'll ever see anyone there, but you must keep checking. Your frequent appearances may be doing more to conserve the fish in that pond than all the people you will ever find in violation put together. If you can learn to pace yourself year in, year out, throughout your career, so that there is not a slump at some point toward the end, you will have persevered.

I cannot end this without using a retired warden I know as an example of what it means to persevere. Warren Adams of Dixfield retired in 1969. The last year he worked, he apprehended the highest number of violators he had ever had in that district, and was high man in his division. At the time, this did not seem so outstanding to me. When he retired, I was assigned to the district for a while, and I knew that this was not one of the higher-producing areas in terms of violations. Now, fourteen years later, and in what has been referred to as the "twilight" of my career, this illustration of perseverance seems to take on even more significance.

To be sure, there are other qualities, such as diligence and humility, that definitely affect the caliber of a game warden's career. These seem to be closely connected with several of the other aspects involved, and hopefully they will take their place among them throughout your career. Earlier I mentioned honesty and integrity. Here is what some people may consider a rather harsh statement: If you did not possess these two basic fundamentals when you became a warden, you may as well hang it all up now. To be an effective game warden or any other type of law enforcement officer without them is impossible.

Now, at some later point, you have completed the long training academy, which all wardens must complete, and have been assigned to a district. If you are like most of us, you will initially go through a period when you feel somewhat out of place in your new uniform. "Damn," you will think to yourself, "I wish I didn't look so brand-new. I wish my hat didn't look like I was fresh out of West Point. Everyone else's equipment looks well broken in, but I look like a department-store mannequin!" You are sure, at every store you go into, that people are scrutinizing you, and thinking, "Well, there's the new warden. I wonder what he'll amount to." When you think all these things, you are absolutely right. It takes some time for the stigma of being "that new guy" to go away. Your new warden brothers will quickly accept you into the fold. What progress you make with the general public, on the other hand, will be up to you. You must work hard to gain the public's confidence and respect. Remember, they will not come to you with the information you need until you have earned their trust. How effective you become in your role as a game warden will rely tremendously on the cooperation the people in your district are willing to give.

After you have been on duty for a while and have gotten your feet wet a few times, you begin to find your niche. Your hat is all wrinkled up now, and has hopefully given you that "been around awhile" look. The awkward feeling you experienced at first has gone away as your confidence in yourself has increased, and now you feel like you belong alongside your fellow wardens. It is a good feeling, this belonging, and you are proud; at least you now have some stories of your own to tell some night at camp. As time goes on, you may wonder, from time to time, what is this almost familial bond that seems to exist among wardens? Is it simply birds of a feather, or something more? I have thought a lot about it, and I am not sure it can—or even needs to—be explained. It just is.

Actually, there are several factors that may have some bearing on it. One of them is that, in many cases, there actually is a family connection. Being a warden is, as I have stated elsewhere, not so much a job as it is a way of life. It is a way of life that wardens' sons become involved in at an early age, as they frequently accompany their fathers on patrol. In many instances, it follows naturally, then, that when they become old enough, they, too, become game wardens.

In the Maine Warden Service, this has occurred many times throughout the years. Retired warden Leonard Pelletier Sr. from St. Francis has to rank above all others in this respect. At one point in his career, Leonard and his three sons, Leonard Jr., Gary, and Roland, plus a brother Maynard, all were wardens at the same time. Without looking into the past records, I can recall seven wardens who had sons that became wardens, all of them while their fathers were still on the force. At least three of these men had more than one son who became wardens. (This also includes several other separate pairs of brothers who are wardens.) Being a warden certainly has become a tradition of sorts in these families.

This may explain the bond of kinship for these particular wardens, but how about the others? The bond is definitely there; it is just perhaps a little harder to convey to a non–Warden Service member. I think possibly there are a number of factors involved.

One thing that stands out, among all wardens, however, is the pride they have in their job. It takes a while to acquire this pride, but slowly, it comes. As you gain experience and learn the ropes, so to speak, you start to develop a deep respect for your fellow wardens and what you all stand for as a team. You learn about wardens who years ago walked the same paths to the same ponds or watched the same fields you now watch. They seemed to have set some pretty high standards, and you feel obligated not to lower them in any way.

You may work for some period of time and not really think about these things. Then, some night after a long, hard day, you and several other wardens get back to a warden camp. It is November, and you have all been searching for a lost hunter. It is raining and raw, and the hunter has been found safe. The stove snaps and pops and quickly heats up the camp. Soon, several pairs of wet socks hung near the stove are steaming, and the unmistakable fragrance of damp boots fills the camp. After supper, you flop on a bunk while your chums sit around and discuss other lost hunters they have found over the years. It is then, while you are lying there on the bunk, thinking about the cold, wet hunter you found earlier, that it suddenly hits you for the first time. As you look around the camp at the traditional red wool warden coats draped over chair backs to dry, and the gun belts hung on nails along the wall, it slowly dawns on you just exactly what being a Maine warden is all about, and you feel good about it. Your career as a warden will be filled with dozens of these experiences. Some will be very good, and inevitably, some will be bad. Either way, it is this combination of shared experiences and camaraderie with your fellow wardens over the years that will help ensure that this family-type bond continues to endure.

It will take you several years to become what can be called a seasoned warden. This is because there are literally hundreds of various situations that can develop during a warden's career, and it takes several years' experience to learn how to handle most of these situations with complete confidence. This has become even more evident in recent years, as wardens' duties have become more numerous and complex.

From time to time, you will undoubtedly hear older wardens say, "I wish we had more time to do fish and game work, like we used to." Well, it would be nice, I agree, but wardens, along with everyone else, now live in a rapidly changing society and have to be much better educated in order to be effective in fish and wildlife conservation. A few short years ago, our predecessors had only fish and game laws to enforce. In recent years, the responsibilities have expanded rapidly to include various environmental laws designed to benefit everyone, not just fish and game. These added responsibilities, along with laws regarding snowmobiles, watercraft, and all-terrain vehicles, have certainly eaten into the time a warden can actually concentrate on only fish and game law enforcement. For the most part, I think, wardens have adjusted fairly well, and have tried to hang on to the real objective involved—that being the protection of fish and game resources.

You probably will not completely comprehend just how much the job of being a warden has changed over the years. Maybe it is not essential that you do, but somehow I think it is important to understand what has brought about these changes. To be aware of what has happened in the past seems to let one view the present, and possibly the future, more objectively. I have spoken to many wardens who worked long before I ever became a warden, and one thing I have noticed is that each generation talks about how things have changed, and speaks longingly of the good old days. One warden, retired lieutenant Charlie Tobie, seemed to put it in excellent perspective, and I would like to use his thoughts as an illustration:

"Compared with many other states, Maine has always had a large number of sportsmen. Hunting and fishing have long been well-established traditions here. Not many years ago, however, these sportsmen utilized relatively primitive equipment in their pursuit of fish and game. Four-wheel-drive vehicles were uncommon, for one thing, and boats and motors were small in comparison to those of today, as well as being by far less numerous. Many

items, such as truck campers and power ice augers, were nonexist-
ent. Another sometimes-overlooked aspect is the fact that while
pulp was being driven down Maine's rivers, it was not necessary to
have and maintain the hundreds of miles of roads that paper com-
panies now have. Most shotguns were either single- or double-bar-
reled. Scope-sighted rifles were rarely seen. For the most part, the
only people one would find on snowshoes were either game wardens, trappers, timber cruisers, or someone who had gone to some
back pond to ice-fish." As Tobie recalls, it was not uncommon during the winter months to snowshoe completely around a small
town and never find any sign of human activity. A warden spent his
winter on snowshoes checking camps, cruising deer yards, and
probably killing a few bobcats.

I think Charlie's observations are extremely meaningful. If
these conditions are compared with the present-day methods in
which sportsmen are able to pursue their interests, it clearly points
out why a game warden's role has changed so drastically.

Some really basic things have not changed, however, and
these are self-evident. There are exactly the same numbers of lakes,
streams, and acres of land in Maine as there were in 1820 when we
became a state. The problem that has been growing ever since then
is that in our steps to enhance our own well-being through advancing technology, we have frequently generated conditions that are
adverse to fish and wildlife habitat. Mother Nature did not include
man in her overall plan, I suspect. Wardens now spend their careers
trying to enforce the fish and game regulations, just as they did
years ago. However, now there are many more players in the game,
and they have much better equipment to play with.

If you are a new warden now, here is an example of what
types of pressure fish and game must contend with: If you are

located in the North Woods, you will notice that new roads are being opened almost daily, and nearly everyone who comes is in a four-wheel-drive vehicle. If it is summer, your usual visitor has a couple of three-wheeled ATVs in the back. If it is winter, he has a trailer with as many as four snowmobiles, and is headed for Chamberlain Lake.

Perhaps your new district is in southern Maine. In early April, you will see several hundred boats in one day on Sebago Lake, nearly all of which are trolling with downriggers and electronic fathometers. On the first Saturday of February in 1985, perhaps you saw between 800 and 1,000 fishermen on Thompson Lake. There were hundreds of vehicles, ranging from four-wheel-drive trucks to snowmobiles and ATVs. The next day you may have patrolled some of the several thousand miles of maintained snowmobile trails throughout Maine while checking the registrations of those you met.

We now take all these various activities for granted, of course, and have no reason not to. The extreme pressures now put on fish and wildlife are numerous and varied. They range from changing land use, such as the reduction of deer habitat through changes in timber harvest methods, to acid rains and other types of pollution.

By now the reader may well wonder, I suspect, what in hell all this has to do with the Maine Warden Service. I think it tends to point out the fact that when one adds up all these things I have mentioned, the game warden's job becomes more important than ever before. His enthusiasm and dedication must continue on at a high level in order to conserve Maine's fish and wildlife heritage and to help ensure future generations of its existence.

In gathering material for this book, I asked other wardens,

young and old alike, what it was that made them decide to be wardens. I also asked them, if they were to read a book about Maine game wardens, what they would like it to convey to the reader. The answer to the first question was generally a love of the outdoors and a desire to help do the obvious task, that being to conserve fish and game. The second question usually took a little more thought. Invariably, though, the conversation drifted back to the deep-rooted dedication to the job, which all Maine wardens seem to share.

Many times, wardens expressed a deep concern that, by and large, a majority of the public had little or no conception about how a game warden viewed his job or how seriously he took it. This is quite true, and maybe I can shed some light on the reasons.

In the course of a warden's work schedule, he is seen by many of the people he deals with only when he wishes them to. He is seen at his house by someone who comes, of course, or is seen driving by your house or maybe going into the courthouse. Very often, he is seen when he does not appear to be working. When he pulls alongside your boat and steps out on the float of a plane to check your license, you know he is around. How about the times he has seen you when you had no idea he was around? You were not breaking the law, that is for sure, or you undoubtedly would have seen him. You have no way of knowing how many long hours he sat in the dark one fall evening at the edge of some field, watching for an illegal hunter, or how many nights he stood shivering on some closed smelt brook. This is the nature of his job. If you knew everything about him, such as where he went, what he did, etc., his effectiveness as a warden would be very limited. He is only able to be in one place at a time. Therefore, it is imperative to have as few people as possible know where this place is going to be, or when.